The Enduring South

The Enduring South

Subcultural Persistence in Mass Society

John Shelton Reed

The University of North Carolina Press
Chapel Hill

Manufactured in the United States of America
ISBN 0-8078-1249-8
Library of Congress Catalog Card Number 74-34271
First printing, August 1975
Second printing, December 1976
Third printing, December 1978
Fourth printing, October 1982

Library of Congress Cataloging in Publication Data

Reed, John Shelton.
    The Enduring South.

    Bibliography: p.
    Includes index.
    1. Southern States—Social conditions. 2. Social surveys—Southern States. 3. Pub-
lic opinion—Southern States. I. Title.
HN79.A13R39   1975   301.15'43'309175   74-34271
ISBN 0-8078-1249-8

Table of Contents

List of Tables

Foreword

The artist, journalist, or historian who ponders the South for a living must at times be haunted, as I am, by the fear that the regional "differences" he traffics in are essentially obscurantist when you get down to it: elegantly so, it may be, but obscurantist all the same.

The Southern novelist may have schooled himself on Tolstoy, the Southern historian on the latest in scientific historiography, the regional political scientist or editorialist may be a master of computer science. Yet, rather to his astonishment, each relies on an asserted differentness that mystifies some, infuriates others, and occasionally gives aid and comfort to sworn political enemies. If this regionalist is Southern-born, as he almost invariably is, he feels the differences in his bones. His is a search for definition and explanation. Yet in the dark of night, he contemplates his profession in terror: Is it perhaps a sort of *trahison des clercs*? Is he dealing in tomfoolery, or raising ancient spirits better left sleeping? Is he a cotton-patch Spengler, a Lysenko of the magnolia groves?

Any student of the South who has known these agonies of self-doubt will find surcease from them in John Shelton Reed's *Enduring South*. Historians and journalists—the latter especially—have not hesitated to speak of a "mind of the South." But their portraits of this mind have rested, for the most part, on unsystematic observation, imaginative rendering of history, intuition, and sometimes sheer bluff. Mr. Reed, speaking from within the citadel of sociology (a discipline regarded by hard-core humanists with ambivalence, at best), has buttressed such imaginings and findings with facts and figures. With sophisticated opinion-sampling techniques, he demonstrates the persistence of a Southern "mind" (or set of mind) and it tallies, for better or worse, with what we had pictured all along. Nor does this regional mind seem a mere anachronism, headed for early extinction. To be sure, Mr. Reed focuses on this mind in limited aspects—as it shows itself in religion (or religiosity), in social ideals and personal life-styles (which in the South remain strikingly parochial), in attitudes toward firearms in the home and the hickory stick in school. But such are crucial to cultural identity.

There is, to my mind at least, a pleasant difference between Mr. Reed's approach to the South and that of the usual regional sociologist. The professional susceptibility of the latter is, in my observation, to treat as "real" whatever regional differences are easily measurable, while dismissing as trifling differences more difficult to measure—like those which form the staple of Mr. Reed's book. He dwells, typically, on such hard data as per capita income, nutrition, the incidence of parasitic disease, urbanization—the nuts and bolts stuff of consumer capitalism—while brushing off as unobjective the historical or "belletristic" modes of perception. His mission, typically, is to wave good-bye to the South, to suggest that it is fading away, or at least being supplanted by one of those "New

Souths" that come and go like French constitutions and theories of the decline of Rome. By and large, then, the social scientist has served the South over the years as a mirror serves a man with a physical deformity—suggesting the need for radical therapy. Yet the grossest deformity, ironically, may be his own: his suggestion, implicit in all this, that the imagination that produces a Colonel Sutpen or a Blanche DuBois is somehow less revelatory of the regional character than the computer that produces that composite of statistics, "the average Southerner."

I know, of course, that the typical sociologist I am depicting is himself a caricature; yet what too many social scientists who have studied the South have failed to see is that no sure correlation exists between condition and attitude. They deny the variety and indeterminacy of the human condition. That is why some of us who take a more than therapeutic view of Southern differences are driven back repeatedly to Cash, or Woodward, or Faulkner, whose lack of system is redeemed by modesty, insight and a sense of historical contingency.

No doubt therapy has been and continues to be in order for the South, in ways obvious to all of us (although one might suppose that Mr. Daniel Moynihan's devastating appraisal of the sociologist-as-therapist in *Maximum Feasible Misunderstanding* had sounded a warning). It may be that Mr. Reed's book has therapeutic implications, but it is valuable quite apart from them. For my part, I am at a loss to say whether the South would be better off if it traded its fundamentalist religion, say, for the commercial secularism that seems to be the prevailing "American" religion. In my view, at any rate, Mr. Reed's findings about the enduring South stand on their own ample, often amusing, terms—the more so, I should say, in view of the fashionable prevailing advice that all regionalists should go baptize themselves in the national mainstream.

In one of her best essays, the late Flannery O'Connor observed that "in the South the general conception of man is still, in the main, theological.... I think it is safe to say that while the South is hardly Christ-centered, it is most certainly Christ-haunted. The Southerner, who isn't convinced of it, is very much afraid that he may have been formed in the image and likeness of God" (to which one must add, the fierce Baptist-Methodist God). For such an observation, Miss O'Connor was licensed by her genius as a storyteller, nothing else. It is pleasant, to me at least, to find that such fancies (as some would call them) may be given statistical foundation. (Not that statistics matter very deeply to the Southerner or his God.)

The same may be said of the perception readily observable in Southern novels at their best and worst: that Southerners are in some sense more prone to violent action than their fellow Americans. Mr. Reed deals modestly with this possibility. From opinion surveys, that is, it may be shown that the Southerner takes a more "permissive" view of firearms and corporal punishment, even when the sample is corrected for regional differences in income, education and rurality. But as Mr. Reed says, in qualification, the data linking these attitudes to "violence" in the larger sense are "embarrassingly tenuous." Never mind. Here again is a certifiable and persistent regional difference, although other Americans are increasingly going in for the pistol and the cudgel.

Without at all compromising the social scientist's exacting standards of inquiry, Mr. Reed renders his findings readable and even entertaining. I pause to note this since he professes a discipline not universally celebrated for the vigor, clarity, or grace of its prose; and all three qualities mark his own.

As for the persisting differences he notes, and whose persistence he probes in the concluding chapter, what shall we say of them? The larger questions are, for me, inspired by Mr. Reed's observation that the South has the "dubious distinction of being in the vanguard of a national trend—it was the most violent region in an increasingly violent nation." Perhaps conquered provinces devour their conquerors, as revolutions do their children. Conceivably Americans today are becoming more tribalistic (more localistic, to use Mr. Reed's term), more given to relaxation and religiosity (as Mr. Reich's "Consciousness III" and the Jesus music flooding the airwaves both suggest), and more tolerant of random violence. Thus trends in the nation at large may draw upon and reinforce what we take to be classic "Southern" attitudes. This is not the place, of course, to inquire what this development portends for all of us. But it is well worth pondering, as one of the many lines of thought provoked by this extraordinarily readable book.

Edwin M. Yoder, Jr.

Greensboro, North Carolina.

Preface

This book is addressed to three distinct sorts of readers: sociologists, students of the South, and that elusive group, "general readers." I run the risk of irritating all three, so I seize this opportunity to address each separately.

My fellow sociologists will see, I trust, that this is intended as a contribution to the branch of our discipline known as "regional sociology." Thirty years ago, calls were heard for attention to the social-psychological aspects of "regionalism," and this is a belated and only preliminary effort in that direction. I also hope that this will be of more general interest to sociologists. I hope to demonstrate that there is, in the South, a regional subculture which has retained much of its integrity. That this should happen in an advanced industrial society where most of the population is far removed from direct dependence on soil and climate is of considerable theoretical interest. Moreover, if a vigorous regional subculture persists in the very country which gave the world the concept of "mass society"—well, at least we should reexamine both the concept and the subculture. Implicit in the text, I hope, is the idea that we need to distinguish between regional subcultures which carry with them a sense of group membership and those which do not. The former, which I argue can be treated theoretically in the same way as ethnic groups, undoubtedly are a hardier variety than the latter.

To historians and other students of the South, who do not feel apologetic about their interest in a particular place and time, I confess my fascination with the American South in the late twentieth century. I hope that there is something to be gained from this monograph by the person interested in the South as *the South*, not as a special case of anything. Much of the text, particularly the last chapter, should be congenial—like an old friend. I apologize for repeating at length what I suspect are commonplaces among Southern historians. Perhaps hearing them stated by a sociologist will be novel enough to be amusing; in any event, I recognize my debt. I have tried to digest the relevant historiography (my dyspepsia may show, from time to time), and if liberties seem to have been taken, it is due to ignorance, and to my sharing T.H. Marshall's (perhaps naive) faith:

It is the business of historians to sift [a] miscellaneous collection of dubious authorities and give to others the results of their careful professional assessment. And surely they will not rebuke the sociologist for putting his faith in what historians write.[1]

Oddly enough, I imagine that historians will find the "historical" parts of less interest than the "sociological" (that is, statistical) parts. Some of the tables in the text show public opinion trends covering as much as thirty years (a very interesting thirty years at that), and may serve to introduce historians to a relatively neglected data source.

If general readers have picked up this book, they have done so for reasons of their own which I cannot begin to anticipate. I can say only that I hope that they find what they are looking for. A couple of "general readers" who were kind enough to read the book in manuscript have independently objected to my use of the comparative method which, they felt, automatically emphasizes the *differences* between South and non-South and obscures *similarities* which may be in some sense more basic or important. I can only reply that that is precisely what it is supposed to do. I share with David Potter the conviction that

Southern studies . . . should not be concerned indiscriminately with everything that occurs within the South; rather they should focus their analysis at points where the conditions of the Southern region differ from those of other regions and should concentrate their attention upon . . . developments which are relevant to these differences. [The student] is dealing with an entity—the South—whose boundaries are indeterminate, whose degree of separateness has fluctuated historically over time, whose distinctiveness may be in some respects fictitious. His job in this complex of uncertainties is to identify and investigate the distinctive features of Southern society.[2]

To each group (not least the general readers), I apologize for pandering to the others by explaining things which are obvious, not explaining things which are abstruse, and failing to elaborate on the "interesting parts"—if such there be.

Acknowledgments

I shall spare the reader my academic biography, but must acknowledge a diffuse and lasting debt to many of my teachers at the Massachusetts Institute of Technology and at Columbia University. If their influence is as evident to my readers as to me, I shall be very pleased.

Among those who have helped with this project, I owe special debts to several. The staff of the Roper Center was invariably helpful and obliging, as was that of the Louis Harris Political Data Center. Without the resources of these archives, of course, this study could not have been done. The Department of Sociology at Columbia University helped with a grant-in-aid for data acquisition and processing, and the staffs of Columbia's Bureau of Applied Social Research (Pnina Grinberg, particularly) and of the Institute for Research in Social Science at the University of North Carolina assisted with data-processing. Mattie Haynes and Elaine Wright aided greatly in the preparation of the manuscript. Glen Elder, Richard Simpson, George Tindall, and Rupert Vance, my colleagues at Chapel Hill, were kind enough to read and criticize an early draft; as were Sigmund Diamond, Jonathan Cole, John Garraty, and James Young, of Columbia. An overriding obligation is to Herbert Hyman of Wesleyan University, whose interest in the project, rigorous attention to detail, and wise counsel sustained me and kept me from many errors.

Chapter 5 is a slightly revised version of my article, "To Live—and Die—in Dixie: A Contribution to the Study of Southern Violence," which appeared in the *Political Science Quarterly* 86 (September 1971), pp. 429-43, and is included here by permission of the Academy of Political Science.

Finally, my wife Dale not only kept our household on an even keel through the months of writing and revising and my attendant tempers, but was of material aid in editing copy. (She dissociates herself, by the way, from my figure of "exorcising the sphinx.") This effort is dedicated to her, and to my daughter Elisabeth—who I hope will work out better than most projects conceived in the North and visited upon the South.

1 "Yes, but Not in the South"

Stephen Potter, in his useful volume, *Some Notes on Lifemanship*, discusses a rejoinder which will serve, with minor modifications, to confound any argument: "Yes, but not in the South." "It is," he observes, "an impossible comment to answer."[1]

Certainly the South has been the region most often the exception to the American rule, and would-be generalizers have often run aground on its peculiarities. Enough have tried to chart a course through this puzzling province to justify amply its frequent characterization as the most studied region in the world. (See the Bibliographical Appendix.) In fact, so many attempts have been made to describe and explain the South that one can sympathize with Helen Hokinson's *New Yorker* matron, who was shown telling a bookstore clerk: "I'm sorry for Mississippi, but I just don't like to read about it." With Rupert Vance's qualification that few feel sorry for Mississippi any longer, the statement might well hold for most readers today.[2] After such an outpouring of words about the South, what could possibly remain to be said?

The Vanishing South

There is an emerging conventional wisdom about the region which deserves scrutiny. The South, runs the refrain, is disappearing: the region is well on its way to becoming "almost indistinguishable from any other region in the country."[3] As usual, journalists have announced this development more colorfully than have social scientists. Harry Ashmore has written *An Epitaph for Dixie*; while *Esquire* magazine, proclaiming that "the South is over," describes for its readers "some of the ways the cracker crumbled."[4] But scholars have also contributed (although more cautiously) to the development of this belief. Leonard Reissman, writing in a symposium with the title "Urbanization and Social Change in the South," has observed that the titles of most recent monographs and symposia on the South have emphasized the South's "emergence," its "transformation," in a word, its *change*—another way of saying its increasing resemblance to the rest of the United States.[5]

Certainly there have been phenomenal changes in the lives of most Southerners during the decades just past. In economic and demographic terms, the South *has* undergone a considerable transformation. To pick one striking statistic: by 1969, Southerners were as likely as any other Americans to have had at least some college education.[6] Although pockets of poverty and ignorance remain, the industrialization for which generations of "New South" thinkers worked has largely taken hold, with dramatic effects on regional differences in education, income, and style of life.[7] For changes of such magnitude in the material conditions of life in the South *not* to affect the attitudes and values which have distinguished Southerners in the past would be virtually inconceivable. Some have gone so far as to argue that "to the extent that the daily occupational and educational environment of the Southerner becomes similar to that of the non-Southerner, the attitudes and values of the two will also become indistinguishable."[8]

Add to the impact of industrialization and urbanization the effects of mass society and mass communication—the whole logic of which, it seems, must be to reduce sectional differences—and there appears to be little reason to suppose that the South—"this sphinx on the American land"—will not be exorcised shortly.[9] Josiah Royce sketched the outlines of the argument (disapprovingly) at the turn of the century:

[B]ecause of the ease of communication amongst distant places, because of the spread of popular education, and because of the consolidation and centralization of industries and of social authorities, we tend all over the nation, and, in some degree even through the civilized world, to read the same daily news, to share the same general ideas, to submit to the same overmastering social forces, to live in the same external fashions, to discourage individuality, and to approach a dead level of harassed mediocrity. . . . [O]ur modern conditions have greatly favored the increase of the numbers of people who read the same books and newspapers, who repeat the same phrases, who follow the same social fashions, and who thus, in general, imitate one another in constantly more and more ways.[10]

It is evident to the most casual observer that the Southern way of life has been substantially reconstructed by these developments. Many of the more picturesque derivatives of rural poverty and isolation have vanished, to the point where undergraduates look puzzled at the mention of pellagra or soil erosion, and John Westbrook can write truthfully of his Louisiana neighbors: "I have positively no firsthand . . . knowledge of one-mule farms, possum and yams, or poor white trash."[11] Nationally-distributed, mass-produced consumer goods guarantee that the clothes worn in Richmond, Virginia, look about like those worn in Richmond, California. Now that air-conditioning has made a flat-on-the-ground, low-ceilinged subdivision house bearable in the Southern climate, the houses being built in the suburbs of Atlanta are indistinguishable from those being built near Detroit. Southerners can take comfort from the fact that the cultural balance-of-payments is not entirely one-sided: a New Jersey radio station broadcasts "the Nashville sound" to greater New York; Southern cuisine (even possum and yams) has experienced a vogue as "soul food"; and Madison Avenue has rediscovered the delights of bourbon whiskey (just as Peachtree Street was getting used to Scotch).

Even the Southern shibboleth of white supremacy—"the cardinal test of a Southerner," according to the distinguished historian U.B. Phillips—has given ground to these powerful nationalizing influences[12] (aided, it is true, by a stiff dose of federal coercion and the South's tradition of exporting its racial problems).[a] One of the most abrupt turnarounds in the history of public opinion polls has been that shown by white Southerners between 1942, when 98% said white and Negro students should go to separate schools, and 1970, when only 16% said they would object to their children going to school with "a few" black children. Data from these same polls show a hardening of non-Southern opinion during the 1960s, with the result that, although a regional difference still persists, that difference is smaller than at any time in the recent past.[13]

No doubt in part as a result of the fading of the "race issue," the historic allegiance of white Southerners to one-party politics is crumbling. Some years ago, Rupert Vance predicted that "some Southerners will become Republicans . . . and others will become better Democrats." He is being proved right. Southern' conservatives, particularly young ones, are increasingly likely to identify themselves as Republicans; and there is a growing body of self-designated liberals—again, particularly among the young.[14] One public opinion expert recently reported: "About half of white Southerners between 15 and 20, who identify with an ideology, call themselves liberals. . . . When blacks are added in there is no significant difference at all between 15-20 year olds [in the South and those elsewhere]."[15]

If the Solid South is coming unglued, if racial discrimination is now to be practiced covertly, if country musicians are playing in Carnegie Hall (and orchestra conductors are eating chitlins), who can doubt that the South is entering an era in which old times there will have been forgotten, and Southerners will have taken on all-American attitudes and values to go with their newfound all-American prosperity and air pollution?

"Is It True What They Say About Dixie?"

And yet. . . . There have been some dissenting voices. The titles of *their* symposia and essays may straddle the fence (*The South in Continuity and Change*, for instance) or come down firmly on the side of continued Southern distinctiveness (*The Lasting South*, even *The Everlasting South*).[16] Some have been cynical enough to observe that the vision of a "New South" has been chronic in the

[a]Here, as elsewhere when I refer to "Southerners" without a qualifying racial adjective, I am following the common usage, in which the referent is *white* Southerners. It is symptomatic of Negroes' exclusion from much of Southern life that they are typically excluded from the very category "Southerner." Also, to avoid repeating the awkward construction "non-South," I shall sometimes refer to the non-Southern United States as "the North." The reader should keep in mind that the contemporary "North" includes the Pacific and Mountain States and much of the Southwest. See the discussion of regional definition in the next chapter.

Southern past.[17] These skeptics have been supported by some recent testimony from a social scientist, Norval Glenn, that regional cultural differences have been decreasing more slowly (if, indeed, they have been decreasing at all) than some have feared and others hoped.[18]

I will try in the chapters following to bring the tools and findings of public opinion research to bear on this question. We shall look closely at North-South differences of three sorts: differences in attachment to the local community, in attitudes toward the private use of force and violence, and in religious and quasi-religious beliefs and practices. These are differences which many observers have claimed exist, and for that reason alone they are worth looking into.

Another reason for selecting these three areas for inquiry is that they seem to me to be at an appropriate level of "importance" for examining the question of the effects of Southern economic development and American mass culture on Southern distinctiveness. They are not as vagrant, responsive to fashion, and derivative from material circumstance as are patterns of consumer behavior.[19] If a Southern regional subculture is persisting, it will be at this level, and not at that of wool hats or mint juleps. On the other hand, unlike Southern racial attitudes and practices, these regional differences have not been seen as *so* important that there has been a concentrated effort to eradicate them. Since the recent history of Southern racial attitudes suggests, a fortiori, that purposive intervention can reduce regional differences, differences subject merely to erosion are of more interest here than those which have been the object of *force majeure.*

Finally, I will argue in chapter 7 that Southern distinctiveness in these three areas arose at the same time, and for the same reasons. The selection may not be as arbitrary as it seems.

These three areas are also, not at all incidentally, areas for which abundant data were available in the archives of old survey data.[20,b]

In chapters 4, 5, and 6, we shall look at evidence of two sorts for the existence of these differences. As evidence for their existence in the past—and prima facie evidence of their present existence—the testimony of scholars (primarily historians) will be examined. The opinion poll data can then be brought forward to tell us whether the traits said to typify Southerners are, in fact, still more frequent among Southerners than among non-Southerners.

The reader may take it for granted that these traits are more frequent among Southerners, in which case the question arises: to what extent are these differences due to the South's lag in urbanization, industrialization, and education? Might not these traits typify rural, uneducated people everywhere, and turn up in regional comparisons simply because of the concentration of such persons in the South? "Test-factor standardization," a technique borrowed from demog-

bSome available, relevant data were not obtained for analysis. For the sake of economy, only surveys which were relatively "rich" in questions of interest were reanalyzed. See the Methodological Appendix for a discussion of the advantages and disadvantages of working with previously collected data, a strategy known as "secondary analysis."

raphy, allows us to remold the South nearer to our hearts' desire and examine the culture of a hypothetical region populated by Southerners who are as educated, urban, and white-collarized as non-Southerners are presently. Whatever differences remain must be due to something other than economic development and urbanization. (See the Methodological Appendix for a description of the standardization technique.) The results of the standardization will give some indication of whether the seemingly inexorable development and urbanization of the South can be expected to obliterate these differences.

Frequently, trend data will also be available, and we can see whether these differences have been attenuated in the recent past. Development of the South has been proceeding apace for at least the last few decades, and the mass culture argument is nothing new. If the South is going to vanish, its disappearing act should have begun by now. The trend data will also give us another basis for projecting, by straightforward extrapolation, to the near future.

Finally, as a by-product of the standardization procedure, we will be able to look at different population strata *within* the South, to see whether some are "more Southern," relative to the corresponding strata outside the South, than others. There has been some speculation, for instance, that city people are pretty much alike, and the bulk of any regional difference will be found among rural populations. As J.O. Hertzler put the question in 1939: "As American population elements move from agriculture to industry, from ruralism to urbanism, from a lower culture level to a higher, does the natural determining influence of region diminish?"[21] We will be able to see whether this is so generally; or, if not, in what respects it is so.

Why South-North Comparisons?

A digression may be in order to explain why the South will be compared to the non-South. The answer may not be as obvious as it seems. After all, many estimable studies of Southern life and culture have been conducted without a comparative dimension at all.[22] And a great many not-so-estimable generalizations about the South are phrased entirely in absolute terms (as when one hears that "Southerners are hospitable," or "bigoted," or whatever).

One reason for including non-Southern Americans as a comparison population is that, on one level, the object of interest in this study is not the South in particular, but the United States, and the variable of interest is regional differentiation, a property of the nation as a whole. A simple measure of this variable is simply the difference between the least typical region (the South) and the rest of the country.[23] How large is the difference? Are the regions converging (and never mind what consensus they are reaching)?

If one takes a less even-handed view, and regards the South as of particular interest, the comparable data for the rest of the United States are still of great value. Any extensive, quantitative study of a population will obviously reveal variation *within* that population. To speak of an attribute as characteristic of the South requires that its frequency in the South be compared to some norm. Lurking in the background of most "non-comparative" studies of the South is an *implicit* comparison—usually to the North—which is unexamined and often dubious. (Herbert Hyman has referred to the conscious use of this strategy as the "pseudo-comparative design" or "fictitious comparison.")[24] Particularly with quantitative data, there must be some method for extracting meaning from a particular figure: Is 60% a lot, or not many? The problem is compounded by the possibility that the absolute figure may be subject to irrelevant seasonal fluctuation, to variation due to question-wording, or to any of a number of other sources of error. By introducing a comparison group, subject to the same factors, and concentrating on the *difference*, these sources of variation can be largely ignored.[25] A great many baselines could be used, but examining the non-South (rather than, say, Bulgaria) is not only efficient use of available data, but—by holding constant those things which Southerners and non-Southerners share, as Americans—makes methodological sense.[26] By looking at the difference between the two, one can isolate the effects of "region" from those of simply being American.

This is not to say that the absolute level of some characteristic in the South is not of interest. Of course it is: it matters a great deal, for instance, whether 90% or 16% of Southerners support segregation. The primary question here, however, is whether Southerners are any *more* likely to show certain characteristics than are other Americans, and the appropriate measure for that purpose is the *difference* between the two populations. In the tables below, that statistic will be emphasized; where we have trend data, we shall be less interested in the component of change shared by all Americans than in whether the North-South difference is increasing, decreasing, or remaining the same.

All of the comparisons shown will be between Southern and non-Southern *whites*. While it would be interesting to examine differences between Southern and Northern Negroes, it would be difficult with these data, since so many Northern blacks are Southern-born and since—particularly in the early polls—the black respondents are not representative of the black population. In any event, the group of particular interest here is white Southerners, and white non-Southerners are the appropriate comparison group since we are interested in the effects of being Southern rather than those of being white.

Outline of the Book

The evidence bearing on regional cultural differences and their persistence will be examined in chapters 4, 5, and 6 (and the impatient reader can skip to those chapters immediately). Chapter 7 is devoted to summary and discussion of those findings. Before turning to these matters, however, some related questions will be addressed.

In the next chapter, we shall consider the question: what is a Southerner? In the first place, what does the variable "Southern-ness" *mean*? Can it be subsumed under some general class of sociological variables? In the second place, how shall we decide, operationally, who is a Southerner and who is not? This last question will lead us into an exercise in regional definition: we shall have to draw the boundaries of the geographic South.

In chapter 3, we shall look at some evidence indicating what Americans perceive to be regional differences. This will obviously have some relation to the actual differences, if there are any, but—particularly in a period of rapid change—the relation may be tenuous indeed. The principal reason for studying the stereotypes of Southerners and non-Southerners held by Americans is simply that these perceptions are of interest in themselves. As W.I. Thomas remarked: "If men define situations as real, they are real in their consequences."[27] The course of sectional relations and personal interactions will be affected as much by perceived differences as by real ones.

2

Southerners: Who, What, and Where

If the Confederacy had made a go of it, the question of who is a Southerner could be addressed as a matter of citizenship, this research billed as a study of "Confederate national character," and this chapter omitted. Since Southerners are not Confederate nationals, however, we must address the question of what they *are*, a question which students of national character can more convincingly (if no more legitimately) ignore. If we are to examine differences between Southerners and non-Southerners, we must have a way of deciding who is which.

"Residence," like "race" and "religion," has been routinely gathered as a "face-sheet" datum by opinion researchers for as long as such research has been done: powerful testimony to its explanatory value. Equally impressive, it is *always* included in sampling controls; perhaps the first criterion for a representative sample is that it be geographically representative. Yet the conceptual status of "region" as an attribute of individuals (not "regions" as geographical entities) remains unclear.[1]

Like race, and like religion in its noncreedal aspects, region is a summary construct. It "often captures (imperfectly to be sure) a set of historical experiences, socialization patterns, life styles, and . . . culture differences."[2] There is an *intrinsic* aspect of region, however, which sets it off from these other face-sheet data. As many "regionalist" scholars have observed, there are good reasons to suppose that the simple fact of residence in a particular area, implying exposure to a peculiar climate, soil, and terrain, will produce distinctive effects.[3] If regional differences in culture and demography exist, residence alone will also determine exposure to these no-less-important "climates."

In the case of Southerners, there seems to be still another factor at work. For many—perhaps most—white residents of the South, the word "Southerners" is not merely a descriptive label for a category which includes them, but the name of a group to which they feel they belong. In sociological terms, "the South" serves not only as a membership group, but as a *reference* group.[4] The use of the variable "region" (frequently dichotomized as "South/non-South") by survey analysts seems to reflect an awareness of this fact. Like religion or race, region (when it is not used simply to cross-tabulate questions which implicate sectional interests) often appears to be used as an imperfect measure of *ethnicity*. Let us examine this assertion a bit more closely.

9

What Is "Southern-ness"?

Lewis M. Killian's book, *White Southerners*, was published recently in a series called "Ethnic Groups in Comparative Perspective."[5] In it, Killian suggests that white Southerners can be viewed fruitfully as an American ethnic group, similar in many respects to Irish-, Italian-, or Lithuanian-Americans. If Killian is right, if most of what we mean by "Southern-ness" can be treated as a special case of ethnicity, several advantages should follow. The conceptual economy will be great; some unobvious implications may be present; and the discomfort experienced by fastidious analysts who have to use the variable should be diminished.

Although the term "ethnic group" usually refers to a "group which is defined or set off by race, religion, or national origin, or some combination of these categories," Milton Gordon has observed that the "common social-psychological referent" of these categories is that all "serve to create, *through historical circumstances*, a sense of people-hood for groups within the United States . . . , a special sense of both ancestral and future-oriented identification with the group" (emphasis added).[6] Although Gordon prefers to consider regional "subsocieties" as independent of and cross-cutting ethnic "subsocieties," I would argue that the Southern regional subsociety may be thought of as roughly coterminous with a Southern ethnic subsociety, and that it differs in this respect from most other regional subsocieties.[7]

Gordon identifies three "functional characteristics" of an ethnic group:

1. It serves psychologically as a source of group identification
2. It provides a patterned network of groups and institutions which allows an individual to confine his primary group relationships to his own ethnic group throughout all stages of the life cycle
3. It refracts the national cultural patterns of behavior and values through the prism of its own cultural heritage[8]

All regional subsocieties serve the second function, virtually by definition. In later chapters, evidence bearing on the third will be examined.

As for the first, some striking data are available. In 1961, Donald Matthews and James Prothro, in the course of a larger study, asked a sample of white Southerners two questions (mutatis mutandis) which had been used earlier to study the "group identification" of Negroes, Catholics, Jews, and union members. They were:

1. Some people in the South feel they have a lot in common with other Southerners, but others we talk to don't feel this way so much. How about you? Would you say you feel pretty close to Southerners in general or that you don't feel much closer to them than you do to other people?
2. How much interest would you say you have in how Southerners as a whole are getting along in this country? Do you have a good deal of interest in it, some interest, or not much interest at all?[9]

A simple index was constructed from these two items, running from zero (low identification) to three (high identification).

By this measure, white residents of the South show a fairly high degree of solidarity, compared to members of the other groups. Table 2-1 reproduces the mean score for each group. The average score for the entire Matthews-Prothro sample is 1.9, the average for those respondents who were raised in the South is 2.0, indicating a level of group identification exceeding that of Catholics and union members, and approaching that of Jews and Negroes.

Can we class Southerners with other "ethnics?" The analogy fits better in some respects than others. Unlike most of the groups more often thought of as "ethnic," white Southerners are not, by and large, recent immigrants or their descendents.[10] (They are, however, like Negroes, *unwilling* Americans—the blacks did not want to come, and the Southerners tried to leave.) We simply do not have data bearing on the important question of whether regional identity makes any difference in interaction: is it a factor, for example, other than through propinquity, in selecting a marriage partner? Although psychological factors like identity and attitudes must have *some* implications for behavior, it is good that they are interesting in themselves, since social psychologists are perpetually rediscovering that their relation to behavior is much less than perfect.[11]

Southerners' differences from the American mainstream have been similar in kind, if not degree, to those of the immigrant ethnic groups. In the aggregate, they have differed demographically—they have been poorer, less educated, less urban. While physical appearance and family name are seldom status cues, accent is. Although Southerners' religion has traveled under the same label as that of non-Southern Protestants, there have been qualitative differences, which will be examined in Chapter 6. They have been, as noted, stereotyped by others and by

Table 2-1
Mean Scores of Various Groups on Index of "Group Identification"

White Southerners	
Total	1.9
Those raised in South	2.0
Other Groups[a]	
Southern Negroes	2.5
Non-Southern Negroes	2.2
Jews	2.2
Union members	1.8
Catholics	1.6
Union household members	1.6

[a]Source: Angus Campbell et al., *The American Voter: An Abridgement*, p. 170. Copyright 1964. Reprinted by permission of John Wiley & Sons, Inc.

themselves. Their degree of cultural difference and their rate of cultural "assimilation" will be treated below. Note that only Southerners, of all American regional groups, meet all of these criteria.

Some are born Southern, some achieve it, and some have it thrust upon them. Southern-ness may be easier to acquire or to shed than other ethnicities, since most of the ethnic status cues can be learned or unlearned with relative ease. This may be an important limitation on the applicability of the ethnic model, since many Southerners—with greater or lesser inadvertence—pass for run-of-the-mill white Protestants once they leave the region, and (although there are no data) it seems unlikely that Southern identity often persists beyond the first generation outside the South, except in enclaves. (My impression is that *non-Southern* identity may last longer in the *South*, partly through choice, and partly not.)

If it is relatively easy for Southerners to "pass," however, the regional base of the group makes it relatively unlikely that most will have occasion to. Other ethnic groups are much more interspersed with other groups, are usually more specialized economically, and may be more likely to be discriminated against. They are, therefore, more likely to have to interact with persons who are not group members, and it is more likely that they will find it advantageous to suppress ethnic cues. White Southerners, on the other hand, residing in the South, may almost never interact with anyone who is not a white Southerner. (Always excepting blacks—the minority's minority; there would seem to be little reason ordinarily, however, for white Southerners to suppress their ethnicity in interaction with blacks in the South.)

It is the high correlation of residence with an ethnicity based on that residence which makes the South, if less than a nation, more than a "region" in the sense in which human ecologists and social geographers use the word. The element of *identity* makes Josiah Royce's definition of a "province" apt: ". . . any one part of a national domain, which is, geographically and socially, sufficiently unified to have a true consciousness of its own unity, to feel a pride in its own ideals and customs, and to possess a sense of its distinction from other parts of the country."[1][2]

Who Is a Southerner?

For some purposes, a measure of "Southern-ness" based simply on residence might be more appropriate than one based on ethnic identification. For the social-geographical study of regional differentiation, for instance, it would make no difference whether ethnic Southerners ceased to be different or became uniformly dispersed over the United States; in either case, differences between the geographic South and the rest of the country would decrease.

Here, however, individuals' ethnicity is clearly of more interest than is the brute physical datum of residence, and there may be better ways to measure the former than by using the latter. The straightforward question "Are you a Southerner?" has much to be said for it, although some respondents would undoubtedly view it as offensive or bizarre. The "Index of Group Identification" offers another approach, although we might wish to distinguish between identification with the group and perceived membership in it.

In any event, when using data collected by someone else, it is necessary to use the measure at hand. In this case, Southern residence must be used as an indicator (however imperfect) of Southern ethnicity. The problem this poses is similar in kind, although probably greater in magnitude, to that presented by accepting interviewer ratings based on skin color as a measure of race.[13] In each case, it might profit us to consider the validity of the quick-and-dirty measure as an indicator of the more elusive variable.

Where Is "The South"?

A prior but related question is the geographical one: where is the South, this region whose residents are to be called "Southerners?" Royce's definition of a province suggests that the answer should be approached along the line of identification—perhaps "where the natives consider themselves to be Southerners" (perhaps with a contiguity provision to include Huntsville). Among the many characteristics which have been used to map the South, however, from mules to non-Ph.D.'s, self-designation has not been one.

This is rather surprising, actually, since the superiority of such a measure for most social-scientific purposes has been generally acknowledged. Howard Odum, for instance, observed that "among the various concepts of a 'region,' one is sociologically most adequate: 'the region is an area of which the inhabitants feel themselves a part.' "[14] In his many writings, Odum frequently distinguished between the region as "an extension of the folk" and "the region determined by technological boundaries or social incidence," stressing that the former was the unit of interest to social science, the latter the basis for efficient planning or administration.[15] In practice, however, Odum and his colleagues were predominantly concerned with planning, and consequently with regional delineation by "technological boundaries or social incidence."[16]

Since we are only given definitions of "the South" in these terms, it will be necessary to consider the correspondence of Southern ethnicity to residence in the region so defined. Before doing so, these methods of regional definition should perhaps be more closely examined. Two general approaches can be distinguished.[17]

The first, that employed by Odum, defines a region as an area within which certain characteristics or phenomena are found extensively and outside of which they are not. Besides mules and Ph.D.'s (of which the South has had many and few, respectively), the South has been defined by its linguistic patterns, plumbing arrangements, intestinal parasites, savings bank deposits, and literally hundreds of other criteria.[18] (Odum alone used more than seven hundred indices in his monumental *Southern Regions of the United States.*[19]) Fortunately for scholars (if not for Southerners) distributions of these phenomena overlap considerably, allowing one to speak of "the South" as a more or less unitary phenomenon.[20]

A second approach to regional definition locates areas which are in some fashion—usually commercially—integrated.[21] Boundaries of the South established in this fashion are roughly similar to those obtained by the method of looking for differentiation.

While each of these approaches is useful for administrative or proto-administrative purposes, both are premature here. If one is concerned with the South as a province, that is, as a self-conscious section, two interesting questions are foreclosed: (1) in what respects and to what extent is the area different from its surroundings? and (2) is the area integrated in various ways? (Defining a region by identity, of course, begs the question of whether a differentiated or integrated population is self-conscious.)

Both sorts of definition, moreover, have another undesirable consequence. If part of the ethnic South becomes healthy and prosperous, or if it becomes commercially dependent on a non-Southern metropolis, it may cease *by definition* to be Southern. (Thus, by Odum's criteria, Texas and Oklahoma, if they ever were Southern, were by the 1930s part of a "Southwestern" region with Arizona and New Mexico.[22]) A population's degrees of identity, integration, and differentiation from adjoining populations are no doubt interrelated, but one does not necessarily imply the others. Each may be used to define a population; the first is clearly preferable here.

Any way of defining the South encounters problems stemming from the fact that "Southern-ness" is very much a matter of degree, for areas as for persons. Some isopleth has to be chosen as "the" boundary: some critical value of the horse-to-mule ratio, some more-or-less arbitrary proportion of self-defined Southerners in the population, and so forth. This problem is compounded by the likelihood that "natural" regional boundaries will not follow state lines. It is often desirable for scholarly or administrative purposes not only to have hard and fast regional boundaries, but to have them accord with existing political boundaries, and most definitions in use yield to these exigencies. Any definition of regions will, of course, obscure the existence of subregional differentiation.

In most of the following analysis, the South has been operationally defined as the eleven ex-Confederate states, plus Kentucky and Oklahoma. This is the definition used by the Gallup organization, and the samples used were drawn with region, defined in this way, as a control. (The National Opinion Research Center's definition of the South is more inclusive. They use the "census South," which adds Delaware, Maryland, the District of Columbia, and West Virginia. In the few tables based on NORC data, this is the definition being used.) To what extent does this definition correspond to the boundaries of "the South" which would be drawn on the basis of self-identification data?

How Well Does Southern Residence
Measure Southern Ethnicity?

Only an approximate answer can be given. The "index of group identification" examined earlier measures one aspect of Royce's definition, that of "consciousness . . . of unity." Since the Matthews-Prothro data were collected from eighteen sampling points scattered around the South, it is possible to examine the geographic distribution of this variable. Figure 2-1 shows, for each sampling point, the median score of respondents on the index.[a] (The number of respondents in each community is indicated in parentheses.) Notice, in the first place, that most areas display a fairly high level of identification with the South (as measured by this index). Despite the small subsamples, the exceptions are where one might expect them to be: the Appalachian subregion, southern Florida, and the Southwest. The belt of high "Southern identification" corresponds approximately to areas of cotton cultivation.

On the basis of these data, and considering the sections of the states being examined, there is no reason to exclude any of the states from the Gallup definition. The situations of Kentucky and Oklahoma remain problematic (since Matthews and Prothro collected no data from them), and Virginia cannot be viewed as conclusively Southern (although one may assume that returns from eastern Virginia would show greater "Southern-ness" than those from the coal-mining area of southwest Virginia). Texas is clearly less Southern than the states to its east, but is quite comparable to North Carolina.

Other data (also suggestive rather than definitive) tap another aspect of Royce's definition: the South's "pride in its own ideals and customs." To the extent that a preference for Southern things corresponds to Southern ethnicity, these data can also be used to get a rough idea of the territorial limits of the South. They have the added advantage of coming from the entire United States (which will show if any states have mistakenly been left out of the South by Gallup's definition) and, since they were collected by the Gallup organization, any biases in their collection will overlap somewhat with biases in the collection of the Gallup data to be analyzed later. Their principal disadvantage is that they cannot be assigned to areas smaller than states, and the state subsamples are not expected to be representative of the states from which they were drawn. That is, we can compute an index score for respondents from Virginia, but those respondents are geographically concentrated within Virginia and are probably

---

[a]The index was computed somewhat differently in table 2-1 and figure 2-1. In the latter, its range is from 0 (low identification) to 4 (high identification).

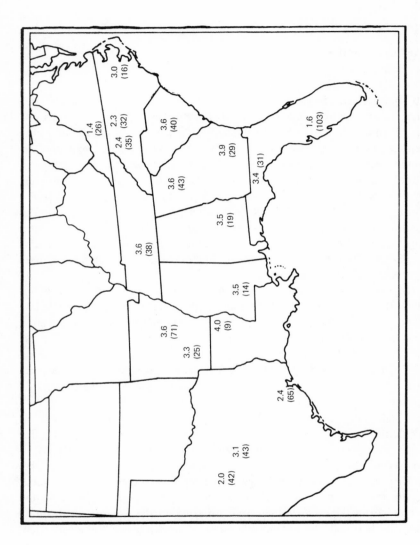

Figure 2–1. Median score on Southern identification index, for eighteen communities.

not representative of Virginia's total population. Since we have seen the considerable intrastate variability in Southern identity, this limitation should be kept in mind. All that can be said of the figure for a particular state is that it is somewhere within the range of figures for different communities within the state. In other words, if the score for Texas is higher than that for Arkansas, all that can be said for certain is that some indeterminable part of Texas is more "Southern" (by this measure, and subject to sampling error) than some part of Arkansas.

The "index of Southern preference" was computed from responses to three items asked of a national sample by the American Institute of Public Opinion (AIPO) in 1957:

1. Now, what do you think about Southern cooking?
2. Do you like the Southern accent?
3. Generally speaking, would you say that Southern women are prettier than those from other sections of the country, or not?[23]

Unconditional approval was scored "1" for each item; any other response was scored "0." This gives a simple index, the number of items unconditionally approved, ranging from 0 to 3.

Figure 2-2 shows the mean score on the index for respondents residing in different states. (The number of respondents from each state is shown at the side of the figure.) Despite the absurdly small samples from some states and the other limitations of those samples, the index scores accord remarkably well with expectation, and with Gallup's definition of the South. If we arbitrarily say that a state qualifies as "Southern" if its average score is greater than one and a half, all of the states in Gallup's "South" (except two from which no data were gathered) qualify; and only one outside (Maryland) does so. The border states and some of the western states are intermediate between the South and the "Old North," while the ordering within the South makes as much sense as could be expected with the small N's on which the means are based.[24] Note that, unlike Matthews' and Prothro's data, these show Virginia and North Carolina to be comfortably Southern, while Texas and Florida are still marginal.

Overall, Gallup's "Southerners" had a mean score of 2.03 (71% approved two or all three items), while the non-Southerners had a mean of 1.03 (only 29% approved two or three). If ethnic Southerners are more likely than others to be partial to Southern food, accents, and women, Gallup's regional division apparently isolates them fairly well.

Sources and Effects of Measurement Error

By operationalizing "Southerner" as "one who lives in one of these states," we are choosing to disregard the fact that, although the correlation is high, there are

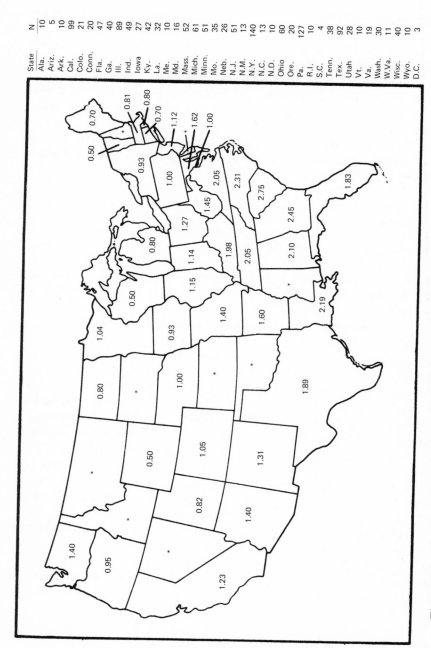

Figure 2-2. Mean score on index of Southern preference, by state of residence. (*No interviews conducted in these states.)

State	N
Ala.	10
Ariz.	5
Ark.	10
Cal.	99
Colo.	21
Conn.	20
Fla.	47
Ga.	40
Ill.	89
Ind.	49
Iowa	27
Ky.	42
La.	32
Me.	10
Md.	16
Mass.	52
Mich.	61
Minn.	51
Mo.	35
Neb.	26
N.J.	51
N.M.	13
N.Y.	140
N.C.	13
N.D.	10
Ohio	60
Ore.	20
Pa.	127
R.I.	10
S.C.	4
Tenn.	38
Tex.	92
Utah	28
Vt.	10
Va.	19
Wash.	30
W.Va.	11
Wisc.	40
Wyo.	10
D.C.	3

many residents of these states who do not consider themselves Southerners and many residents of other states who do. One obvious source of this problem is migration. Although birthplace may be at least as imperfectly correlated with ethnicity as is present residence, the magnitude of the error introduced by migration can be estimated by considering that 12% of all white native American residents of the (census) South were born outside the region and 6½% of native white residents of other regions were born in the South (1960 figures).[25] If all migrants retained identification with their region of birth, about 8% of the total population would be misclassified, not an alarming level of error.

Other sources of misclassification stem from the limitations of the notion of region. The rather arbitrary choice of an isopleth, the extension or truncation of regional boundaries to square them with state lines, the ignoring of internal variation—all will act to rope non-Southerners into the South and to exclude Southerners from it.

Fortunately, unless something very odd is going on, the effects of measurement error are relatively benign. By and large, any error which is present can be expected to *reduce* the measured difference between "Southerners" and "non-Southerners." This will be the case unless those Southerners misclassified as "Northerners" are more "Northern" than the Northerners correctly classified, or those Northerners misclassified as "Southerners" are more "Southern" than the real ones. For instance, if ethnic Southerners really are more churchgoing than the aggregate of other Americans, misassignment will result in a smaller observed North-South difference than would be found with more accurate measurement, *unless* non-Southerners who live in the South are particularly rigorous churchgoers, or Southerners living outside the South are particularly lax.

In general, the sources of measurement error discussed above should result in the misclassification of persons who are, in the aggregate, intermediate between Southerners and non-Southerners in most respects. Hyman and Sheatsley have shown that this is true for migrants, for instance, with respect to racial attitudes, and further analysis of the indices of "Southern identification" and "Southern preference" shows migrants intermediate on these variables as well.[26] Figures 2-1 and 2-2 show that the residents of border states and marginal areas within the Southern states (other candidates for misclassification) are similarly "in-between."

If one feels that "Southern-ness" is not perfectly measured by Southern residence, and if those persons for whom the measurement is wrong display this general pattern, one may assume that the regional differences which do show up understate the actual differences between "real" Southerners and other Americans.

3 "The South of the Mind": Regional Attitudes and Stereotypes

Many Southerners, we have seen, say that they "feel closer" to some people than others, simply because these people are fellow-Southerners. In its extreme form, this might be called ethnocentrism, and the other side of *that* coin—hostility toward those who are not members of the group—deserves inspection. If it appears that many Americans are prepared to dislike others, knowing only that they come from another part of the country, it will surprise neither the student of American history (who has seen it all before) nor the student of ethnic relations (who has seen stranger criteria).

Sectionalism at Mid-Century

Since sectional ill will has played such a prominent part in the history of the United States (even in eras of good feeling it seems merely to have been dormant), one might expect it to have been tagged as a fundamental "social indicator" and monitored from time to time. One would be mistaken: I have been able to locate only one survey which has explicitly measured sectional animosity.

In 1957, respondents to the Gallup Poll were asked: "What do you think of Southerners [for Southern respondents, "Northerners"] generally?"[a] Table 3-1 shows the pattern of responses. By this measure, Northerners' attitudes toward Southerners may be slightly less favorable than Southerners' attitudes toward them. *Extremely* negative responses, however, may be more frequent among Southerners. Eighteen percent of the Southern respondents, when asked what they liked least about the North, passed up the climate to say something unfavorable about the people; only 8% of the non-Southerners said that Southerners were the worst thing about the South (although another 21% said segregation was what they liked least, which may imply an unfavorable evaluation of those who practice it).[1]

In any event, the overwhelming preponderance of favorable attitudes in both regions (particularly if the "no difference" responses are viewed as favorable) suggests that sectional antagonism was not a major cause for concern—in 1957, at least.

With an issue as submerged as this one seems to have been, perhaps it is not surprising that further analysis of these data reveals only slight associations be-

---

[a]Some evidence for the validity and generality of this measure is given by its correlation, in the North, with score on the "index of Southern preference" (see the preceding chapter; gamma is 0.36 for those who gave an evaluation of Southerners). Southerners' opinions of Northerners are less strongly related to their taste for Southern food, speech, and women (gamma = 0.15).

21

Table 3-1

"What Do You Think of Southerners [or Northerners] Generally?": Responses of Southerners and Non-Southerners

	Southerners' Opinions of Northerners	Non-Southerners' Opinions of Southerners
Favorable	48%	45%
No difference between North and South	12	10
Miscellaneous, mixed	2	3
Unfavorable	17	23
Don't know, no answer	22	18
TOTAL	101%[a]	99%[a]
(N)	(347)	(1121)

[a]Totals differ from 100% due to rounding error.

tween sectional feeling and such variables as education, occupation, and urban or rural residence. Students of public opinion have argued that, in general, if an issue is not a topic of contention, persons respond to it on the basis of their idiosyncratic experiences and beliefs. Only when an issue becomes salient do they begin to line up according to their locations in the social structure.[2]

In the present case, anti-Southern sentiment among non-Southerners has about the same geographic distribution as low scores on the "index of Southern preference" (figure 2-2, above). The relatively strong dislike expressed by New Englanders can be shown to be concentrated among New England *Republicans*, probably a residual manifestation of traditional sectional feeling. "Misonotism" (a coinage suggested by a classicist friend, and offered with surpassing diffidence) is slightly more prevalent in the small towns of the North than in large cities or rural areas, and is somewhat more common among educated Northerners than among uneducated ones. Anti-Northern feeling, on the other hand, is found most often among *uneducated* Southerners, and more in the rural South than in Southern towns and cities.[3]

One way a person could generate an opinion of white Southerners, if he has no socially-defined "right" way to feel and has little direct experience to go on, would be to build on whatever attitude he has toward black people.[4] This reasoning makes a plausible hypothesis of Gunnar Myrdal's belief that, "in general, a friendly attitude toward the South carries with it unfavorable views toward Negroes. . . ."[5] Tables 3-2, however, offers only slight support for this notion. Whatever the situation among editorialists and politicians, some members of the general public have their own sorts of consistency: many like everyone, others do not care much for Southerners *or* Negroes.

One factor which does seem to have something to do with sectional hostility is exposure to the other region. Table 3-3 shows that, among Northerners, in-

Table 3-2
"If You Lived in the South, Would You Support Segregation?": Responses of Non-Southerners, by Attitude Toward Southerners

Attitude Toward Southerners	% Who Would Support Segregation[a]	(N)
Favorable	46%	(506)
Unfavorable	39%	(259)

[a]"Don't know" responses included in percent bases.

Table 3-3
Attitudes Toward Residents of Other Region, by Exposure to the Other Region, for Southerners and Non-Southerners

Exposure	Ratio of Positive to Negative Evaluations	% "Don't Know"
Attitudes toward Southerners of Non-Southerners		
Born in South	2.31	2
Travelled in South, not born there	2.26	8
Never been in South	1.55	32
Attitudes toward Northerners of Southerners		
Born in North	7.67	9
Travelled in North, not born there	2.42	14
Never been in North	2.50	32

creased exposure to the South is associated with favorable attitude toward Southerners. The difference between Northerners who have travelled in the South and those who have not may be misleading, however, since travel is at least partly a matter of choice, and those with negative attitudes toward Southerners are presumably less likely to sojourn among them. For Southerners, though, travel in the North seems to make little difference: if anything, those who have been North like Northerners less than those who have not. Northern-born residents of the South display an amazing fondness for their ancestral group, much more than Southern-born migrants show for theirs. It is hard to say why this should be; the two groups must have had different reasons for migrating, or different experiences after doing so.

The data also show an encouraging reluctance on the part of many respondents to engage in blanket judgment. The proportion of respondents who "don't know" is quite large (for a sample from the United States), and the "no difference" category includes some who said such things as "People are the same—

some good, some bad everywhere."[6] The column of "don't know" responses in table 3-3 shows that those who might be expected to know least are the least likely to express an opinion—usually a desirable state of affairs.

Nevertheless, substantial majorities, even of Northerners who have never visited the South and of Southerners who have never left it, are prepared to deliver a general approval or condemnation of the inhabitants of the other region. This suggests that most Americans have at their grasp some regional stereotypes, that they are capable of perceiving Southerners and (by implication, at least) Northerners as possessing "typical" characteristics which can be evaluated. Let us turn to an examination of those perceptions.

"That's What I Like/Dislike
About the South": Regional Imagery

Dozens of characteristics have been advanced as setting Southerners and their way of life apart from the rest of America. Through good times and bad, whatever else may have been in short supply, Southerners have never suffered for lack of generalizations about their characters and cultural traits.[7] These generalizations have ranged from the informed judgments of disinterested foreigners to expressions of prejudice (pro or con) of the rankest sort; and it has not escaped notice that many supposed "Southern traits" seem, on the face of it, mutually exclusive.[8] The accuracy or inaccuracy of these characterizations is, however, beside the point: we want to know whether there is widespread agreement on how Southerners differ from other Americans and—if so—what those differences are seen to be.

The data we have are only fragmentary, but the picture they give us is so familiar that there can be little doubt that it is a true likeness. The original questionnaires for the Gallup study analyzed above were not available, so it cannot be known for certain exactly how the respondents answered questions about what they liked most and least about the South (or North) or what they thought of Southerners (or Northerners) generally. Moreover, unqualified approval or disapproval of Southerners (or Northerners) was not followed in the interview with a request for elaboration. Some respondents volunteered characterizations, however, and these responses were grouped into several categories by the survey organization. The categories were labelled with examples of the responses coded in each. From these category labels, we can extract a number of terms which were used by Northerners to describe Southerners, and vice versa. These terms are listed in table 3-4.

If we ignore the terms common to both characterizations as probably simple expressions of approval or opprobrium (although an interesting question is why these particular words should be used), and ignore for the moment the evaluative component of the words, we see that there is a surprising degree of consensus on what the differences between Northerners and Southerners are. The grouping of

Table 3-4
Descriptive Terms Used by Respondents to Characterize Southerners and Northerners[a]

Applied to Southerners by Non-Southerners	Applied to Northerners by Southerners
friendly[b]	friendly[b]
hospitable[b]	hospitable[b]
polite[b]	polite[b]
nice[b]	nice[b]
unethical[b]	unethical[b]
take life slower	activity of people
don't worry as much	alive
	ambitious
lazy	
shiftless	fast pace
unambitious	
(references to)	
tradition	better educated
culture	good standards
speech	
backward	immoral
ignorant	not religious
low-class	
uneducated	
corrupt	
insincere	impolite
	not hospitable
intolerant	make issue of segregation
bigoted	hypocritical attitude
segregationist	about segregation
	superior attitude
	belittle South
	ridicule [South? Southerners?]

[a]Terms are taken from code labels. See text for caution.
[b]Appear in both characterizations.

terms is rather arbitrary, but note that both groups see Southerners as less *active* (references to pace, laziness, ambition or the lack of it), more *traditional* in outlook (references to Northern education and irreligion), and more *mannerly* (hospitality and politeness were more frequently attributed to Southerners, and nobody called Southerners impolite).

An interesting exception to this pattern of shared perceptions is that Northerners see Southerners as "intolerant," "bigoted," and "segregationist," but Southerners (at least in this sample) do not respond by referring to Northerners as integrationists or miscegenationists (although there are some choice terms in the vernacular that could have been applied). Rather, Southerners accuse Northerners of hypocrisy—implying that they are segregationists, too, *really*—or object to their "making an issue" of segregation.

Aside from this, however, Northerners and Southerners agree about many of the differences between them, although these differences are evaluated differently. To complicate matters a bit, the same perceived difference may be evaluated differently by different persons within either region. It is clear that there is at least a minority in each region which views residents of the other region as superior in some respect. Some Southerners, at least, agree with the Northerners who regard Southern lassitude as indicating lack of ambition; while some Northerners envy the supposed lack of worry and the slower pace which other Southerners see as a Southern virtue. A similar situation prevails with respect to Northerners' education and "standards." The "moral alchemy" of the situation is simple: one man's languor is another's laziness; one's politesse, another's insincerity.[9] The same perceptions can, with minor variations in emphasis, be used to support diametrically opposed attitudes.

These data come from an excellent sample, but the measurement of perceptions is less than satisfactory. Some other data, much more adequately measured, but from a much less representative sample, serve to reinforce the impressions gathered from these data, and fill in some of the gaps. In particular, we can examine Southerners' perceptions of themselves, a subject touched so far only by implication, from their stereotypes of Northerners.

As part of a larger study, forty-seven white Southern college students were given a list of eighty-four traits and asked to indicate which were "typical" of "white Southerners" and which of "white Northerners."[b] Table 3-5 shows the difference in attributions of traits to each of these groups.

The perceptions held by these college students in 1970 are very similar to those reported by the national sample in 1957. The conservative, tradition-loving, conventional Southerner (perhaps merely lazy or stubborn) is seen as opposed to the aggressive, radical (or industrious, progressive, ambitious, alert, efficient) Yankee. The courteous, generous Southerner regards the latter as loud, rude, and mercenary. Some of these students see Yankee sophistication and in-

---

[b]The study was undertaken, in collaboration with Glen H. Elder, as a replication of the study reported in Daniel Katz and Kenneth Braley, "Racial Stereotypes of One Hundred College Students," *Journal of Abnormal and Social Psychology* 28 (October-December 1933): 280-90. The subjects, undergraduate students in an introductory sociology course at the University of North Carolina, Chapel Hill, were asked to characterize the same groups used by Katz and Braley, then "white Southerners" and "white Northerners." An appended "personal data" sheet asked: "Do you consider yourself a Southerner?" Those who said they did not (eight subjects) were excluded from the analysis. (Their responses did not diverge markedly from those of the Southerners.) There were no black students in the class.

Table 3-5
Difference in Attribution of "Typical Traits" to Northerners and Southerners by 47 White Southern College Students

Number Ascribing Trait to Southerners Minus Number Ascribing It to Northerners	"Southern Traits"	Number Ascribing Trait to Southerners Minus Number Ascribing It to Northerners	"Northern Traits"
+30	conservative	−19	industrious
+28	tradition-loving	−18	sophisticated aggressive
+22	courteous	−15	progressive
+20	loyal to family ties	−12	conceited ostentatious (showy)
+18	conventional generous		argumentative
+15	lazy faithful	−11	rude
		−10	materialistic
+14	very religious		loud
+12	ignorant	− 9	ambitious arrogant
+11	stubborn extremely nationalistic		deceitful
	jovial	− 8	mercenary
		− 7	intelligent
+10	honest		scientifically-minded
+ 8	witty		efficient
	kind		persistent boastful
+ 7	superstitious		
	sensitive	− 6	radical sportsmanlike
+ 6	naive		
	revengeful	− 5	methodical
	straightforward		alert evasive
+ 5	stolid		suspicious
	pleasure-loving		
	happy-go-lucky		

between +5 and −5: shrewd, sly, meditative, imaginative, stupid, unreliable, treacherous, cowardly, cruel, grasping, quarrelsome, gluttonous, pugnacious, individualistic, talkative, suave, slovenly, reserved, quiet, ponderous, impulsive, quick-tempered, suggestible, passionate, sensual, humorless, neat, imitative, frivolous, gregarious, practical, musical, artistic, physically dirty, brilliant telligence as reflecting unfavorably on Southern naiveté and ignorance; others see Southerners as straightforward and honest, Northerners as deceitful and evasive—and arrogant, conceited, ostentatious, and boastful to boot (echoes of the "superior attitude" resented by some of the Gallup respondents).

Earlier in the study, these students had been asked to characterize "Americans." For each group, the students were asked to indicate the five "most typical" traits. Table 3-6 shows the "most typical" traits of Americans generally, of white Southerners, and of white Northerners. Remarkably, the image of "Americans" held by these Southern students is virtually identical to their stereotype of "white Northerners" and bears almost no resemblance to that of their own group. If this rating had been done by Northern students, the resemblance between Americans and Northerners could easily be explained. It should be emphasized that the raters were *Southerners*. (Note that the materialism and intelligence attributed to both Northerners and Southerners lead the list of "American" traits. One can but wonder what Americans *are* "gluttonous" and "scientifically-minded"—"typical American traits" characterizing neither Northerners nor Southerners.)

The regional stereotypes these students hold are not at all vague, imprecise, or evanescent. There was widespread agreement on what traits typify Northerners and Southerners—more agreement, in fact, than on "typical Negro traits."[c] Also, although the survey evidence indicates that regional stereotyping is not a universal in American society, *none* of the subjects in this small study refused to characterize Northerners or Southerners, or indicated an inability to do so.

Stereotype Longevity

The idea that Southerners were somehow a distinctive people appears to have flowered in the antebellum period, nurtured both by native defenders of the "Southern way of life" and by Yankee detractors. The different purposes of these two sorts of propagandists produced at least two distinct public images of the South.[10] Although the proportions and coloring were quite different, these two stereotypes shared many of the same details. *Harper's Weekly* likened Southern civilization to "a mermaid—lovely and languid above, but ending in bestial deformity."[11] While some emphasized the loveliness and languor and others the fundament of violence, bigotry, ignorance, and oppression, all but the most rabid partisans acknowledged the existence of the whole creature. As we have seen, much the same situation exists today. Defenders and detractors share

[c]A measure of "definiteness" of a stereotype is the least number of items which must be taken to include half of the choices of "most typical traits." Its range is from 2.5, for perfect agreement, to 42, if all raters respond at random. (Note that a high score, indicating low "definiteness," may be due to individual confusion or to interrater disagreement.) The "definiteness" scores for the stereotypes of blacks, Northern whites, and Southern whites held by these students were 16.5, 8.6, and 9.2, respectively.

Table 3-6
"Most Typical Traits" Most Frequently Ascribed to "White Southerners," "White Northerners," and "Americans," by 47 White Southern College Students

White Southerners		White Northerners		Americans	
Percentage Ascribing Trait	Trait	Percentage Ascribing Trait	Trait	Percentage Ascribing Trait	Trait
51	conservative	49	industrious	70	[a]materialistic
40	tradition-loving	38	[a]materialistic	45	[a]intelligent
			[a]intelligent		industrious
30	conventional				
		30	progressive	32	pleasure-loving
26	courteous				
		23	sophisticated		
23	generous			30	progressive
		21	aggressive		
21	[a]intelligent			26	ambitious
		17	arrogant		
19	pleasure-loving		loud	23	scientifically-minded
	lazy	15	rude		
			ambitious	19	imaginative
17	kind		conceited		aggressive
	honest				extremely nationalistic
	[a]materialistic	13	ostentatious (showy)		
15	faithful			15	ostentatious (showy)
	loyal to family ties	11	alert		
			mercenary		
				13	sportsmanlike
13	stubborn	9	boastful		
	ignorant		deceitful	11	individualistic
	extremely nationalistic		evasive		
			efficient		
			imaginative	9	sophisticated
9	very religious		individualistic		gluttonous
	stupid		radical		
	naive				
	straightforward				
	sportsmanlike				
	shrewd				

[a]attributed to both Northerners and Southerners

many perceptions; each might accuse the other not of fabrication, but of distortion.

Early sectional imagery has been ably discussed in the historical literature, and I shall do no more here than observe that many elements of the modern stereotypes seem to have already existed, full-blown, before the Civil War. Then as now the stereotypes were a composite of accurate generalization and more dubious belief.

The paramount characteristic of Southerners, in the view of twentieth-century Americans, seems to be their relative (if only relative) lack of ambition, energy, and industry. This belief is so pervasive and so firmly lodged in the public mind that it has supposedly affected the location of plant sites, and an entire scholarly monograph has been devoted to it.[12]

We find this generalization fully elaborated in the writings of two antebellum travellers. Frederick Law Olmsted, reflecting in a New York newspaper on his experiences in the South, claimed "the grand distinction" between Southerner and Northerner to be that the "Southerner has no pleasure in labor except with reference to a result. He enjoys life itself. He is content with being."[13] He felt that, fortunately for their slaves, Southerners were of too "careless, temporizing, *shiftless* disposition" to fully exploit them. "The calculating, indefatigable New-Englander, the go-ahead Western man" would have been more demanding.[14] Olmsted's conclusions were essentially those of the French observer, Alexis de Tocqueville. Contrasting the areas north and south of the Ohio, Tocqueville remarked that the Ohioan

regards temporal prosperity as the principal aim of his existence; . . . his acquisitive ardor surpasses the ordinary limits of human cupidity . . . and his avidity in the pursuit of gain amounts to a species of heroism.

The Kentuckian, on the other hand

scorns not only labour, but all the undertakings which labour promotes; . . . his tastes are those of an idle man; . . . he covets wealth much less than pleasure . . . ; and the energy which his neighbor devotes to gain, turns with him to a passionate love of field sports and military exercises. . . .[15]

Whether viewed as a quasi-aristocratic distaste for bustle, or as lethargy indicative of malnutrition, hookworm, and poor character, this trait has clearly been one constant element in the mental construct "Southerner."

A related cluster of "Southern traits" includes such items as traditionalism, conservatism, "backwardness." (On the fringes of this cluster are other "folk culture" traits: religiosity, familism, and the like.) Much of this is implied by the observation that Southerners are more content with their circumstances, but, in general, this aspect of the Southerner's supposed character seems less outstanding in the antebellum period (although some proslavery writers tried to emphasize the "stability" of Southern society and its continuity with the past).[16] Some adumbrations of this aspect of the stereotype can be found: Olmsted, for instance, remarked that "The Southerner ... is greatly wanting in hospitality of mind, closing his doors to all opinions and schemes to which he has been bred a stranger. ... He naturally accepts the institutions, manners and customs in which he is educated, as necessities imposed upon him by Providence." The elaboration of this trait and its elevation to a prominent place in the stereotype however, seem to have come somewhat later.[17]

On the other hand, the image of Southern hospitality and mannerliness which seems to be prevalent in the twentieth century was quite well-developed in the nineteenth. Olmsted wrote of the Southerner's "ready, artless and superficial benevolence, good nature and geniality," noted that "guests [are] usually exceedingly welcome" and that Southerners were "ready and usually accomplished in conversation."[18] (Shrewd observer that he was, he was aware of the element of inscrutability which a code of manners imposes on interaction: " ... it has not appeared to me that the Southerner was frank as he is, I believe, commonly thought to be."[19] Politeness and "sincerity" coexist uneasily as virtues.)

One very prominent element of the antebellum Southern stereotype does not appear at all in the twentieth-century data. In 1861, a young poet wrote to his mother that "the *character* of Southerners has become daily more domineering, insolent, irrational, haughty, scornful of justice."[20] These traits—confidence, power, pride, threat—were widely perceived in the North at the time as characteristic of Southerners. As Howard Odum observed, this is no longer so: latter-day fire-eaters are seen as blustering and vaguely comic figures.[21] The adjectives "arrogant," "ostentatious," "conceited," and "boastful" turn up in our analysis, but they are attributed by Southerners to *Northerners*.

The Ethnic Analogy Reconsidered

George Tindall has written of how the "moonlight and magnolias" version of the South purveyed by popular literature and popular music at the turn of the century gave way to the "Benighted South" (moonlight replaced by moon*shine*) more familiar to modern readers.[22] The latter is still the dominant theme in most treatment of the South by the mass media, and there is some fine irony in the image of Southerners they present: it is similar to the stereotype which many whites hold of blacks.[23] The irony is compounded when we read of a performance by the all-black Negro Ensemble Company that "The white [Southern] townsfolk, all of them played by members of the N. E. C. in whiteface and with cracker accents, are a stupid, shiftless, and highly comical bunch, and watching them try to cope with the simplest of chores affords great delight."[24] The tables no doubt turn sweetly, but the description is hauntingly familiar. To complete the picture, we need only to discover a morbid fascination with the exotic sexuality of Southern males—and, in some effete New England literary circles, one scholar has located even that.[25] If the Southern comedian "Brother Dave" Gardner had ever founded his "National Association for the Advancement of White Trash," its work would be cut out for it. (The crowning touch is that the stereotype white Southerners have of Northerners is similar to that which Northern Negroes have of their white neighbors: "ambitious, sticking together, businesslike, deceitful and tricky, feeling superior," and so forth.[26])

Although Southerners may, of late, have fared worse at the hands of the media than have members of the more established minority groups, the general Northern public has been more cordial.[27] Intersectional attitudes seem at present to be predominantly favorable, or at least neutral—and a Southerner was even elected President recently (although, to be sure, the circumstances were unusual).

Nevertheless, both social and psychological bases exist for a resurgence of sectional animus, should the occasion arise. We have seen that a substantial minority of Americans are able and willing to express dislike for others, given only the fact of their residence. More importantly, perhaps, perceptions of regional differences exist and are widely shared. These perceptions have been quite consistent across time (certainly for the last generation or so), and they are sufficiently ambiguous to serve (as they have served) as a basis for either favorable or unfavorable evaluation. Some of these perceptions, at least, have some basis in fact and, in time, as the facts change, these perceptions may respond. There is little reason from the historical record, however, or from the experience of other groups, to suppose that they must—or that they will not be replaced by other perceived differences.

Of course, the facts may not change. There may be real and enduring cultural differences between Southerners and other Americans. We shall turn to that question next.

4

"Down Home": Southern Localism

The "way of the South," Howard Odum wrote, "has been and is the way of the folk. . . . The culture of the South is the culture of the folk."[1] The idea that "folk culture" (*Gemeinschaft*, in its sociological incarnation) has survived in the South is an attractive one, since it seems to explain—or at least label—many of the peculiarities of the regional culture.[2] One of these peculiarities is a pervading *particularism*: in the South, some have said, persons are viewed as less interchangeable, more as individuals than as performers of specialized roles.[3] Places are less interchangeable, too: home is where the heart is, not just "anyplace I hang my hat." Marion Pearsall has observed that, in the South, "it is the concreteness of life that is valued, the particular locations and the particular possessions," and many others have remarked the Southern attachment to homeplace.[4] Southerners seem more likely than other Americans to think of their region, their states, and their local communities possessively, as *theirs*, and as distinct from and preferable to other regions, states, and localities.

Southern Local Loyalties

The idea of American sections—subnational entities more inclusive than states—antedates the Civil War, as does, apparently, the greater tendency of Southerners to think in sectional terms.[5] The experience of war, defeat, and Reconstruction no doubt reinforced this tendency by giving Virginians and Texans the "something in common" which may have been largely illusory before. (The war also left the South as the only American section with its own flag, anthem, and holidays.) The politicians of the South have been uniquely able to spot the sectional implications of issues, and it is striking that the two twentieth century American intellectual movements which have most strongly emphasized the existence and desirability of regional distinctions—the Agrarianism of Ransom, Warren, Tate, and their associates, and the Regionalism of Howard Odum and his colleagues—had their beginnings and most of their impact in the South.[6] We may surmise that Southerners think of their region more often and are more rooted in it than Midwesterners or New Englanders.

Even within their region, however, and sometimes to the region's detriment, Southerners have displayed great loyalty to their individual states. A regional difference in state sentiment appears to have existed in the antebellum period: an exasperated Northern senator once berated his Southern colleagues for always referring to themselves as "Virginians" or "Carolinians," asking whether all were not Americans together.[7] His rhetorical question was answered after Sumter, when Southerners' loyalties were put to the test, and most went with their states.[8]

To this day, the phrase "states' rights" sounds odd in any accent but Southern. While this principle has yielded to expediency at times, as when Southerners desired a fugitive slave law or prohibition, Southerners seem to be jealous of the rights of *their* states and to define issues in these terms more often than most Americans. They seem to see their states more clearly as bodies politic, and to have stronger feelings about them. Dwight MacDonald may have been inadvertently revealing his parochialism when, proposing to redraw state lines in a more "rational" (utilitarian) manner, he wrote:

My hunch . . . is that most Americans don't have strong emotional State ties . . . and that they would therefore accept a revision of the map which would promise functional improvements.[9]

Such proposals are seldom heard in the South, in part, no doubt, since the region does not yet have the great trans-state conurbations of the Northeast, but also perhaps because such programs would be regarded as political vivisection. As Albig wrote, prophetically, in 1939:

Organization of attitudes, loyalties, and opinions about state symbols, such as flags, mottoes, seals, songs, birds, flowers, popular names, and the like, has been common in American history. . . . Under the guidance of economists and various specialists preoccupied with areas, regions, and other nonpolitical subdivisions, the scholar is likely today to underestimate the vitality of state concepts in the popular mind, especially in the South. . . . Apparently [the waning of local and regional influences on opinion] is not occurring so rapidly as many social theorists anticipated. Man does not move rapidly into the great society.[10]

In support of these observations, we have some recent evidence that Southerners pay relatively more attention to state politics, at the expense of national and international affairs, than other Americans.[11]

Within their states, Southerners often align themselves politically in an "uplands-tidewater" pattern, reflecting the importance of locality at this level as well.[12] (Although intrastate sectionalism exists in non-Southern states, it seems more often there to be basically an urban-rural division.[13]) One frequent exception to this pattern—the "friends and neighbors" vote, whereby a county or two deviates from its traditional alignment to support a favorite son—is not an exception at all, if the persistence of sectional patterns is viewed as a manifestation of local loyalties.[14] A peculiar attachment to local communities may also perhaps be discerned in the work of Southern writers of fiction and verse, who, until recently, generally followed Booker T. Washington's advice to Southern

Negroes and cast down their buckets where they were.[15] Obviously a writer must write about what he knows (although Hemingway did not dwell on Oak Park, Illinois); perhaps the remarkable thing is not that so many Southern writers have written about the South, but that so many have chosen to live there.

Each of these subnational loyalties—to community, to state, to region—could be called a form of parochialism. However, the sociological term *localism* seems preferable, since "parochialism" implies an indifference toward the larger world which "localism" may not.[16] Localism may reflect limited experience and narrow horizons, but it may also be a manifestation of geographic particularism—an appreciation of the qualities of one place as opposed to others.

If localism refers only to an orientation toward one's immediate community, it is too narrow a term for what people mean when they speak of a Southern "sense of place." From the standpoint of a regional planner, however, state loyalties may be viewed as "localistic"; in an international context, national patriotism may be seen as localism. In ordinary circumstances, these various sorts of localism are not mutually exclusive; in fact, they may well cumulate and reinforce one another.[17] Thus Southerners, who have, by hypothesis, stronger ties than others to their region, states, and towns, seem in this century to have been at least as patriotic as anyone else.

"The Old Folks at Home" As Normative
Reference Individuals

One aspect of an attachment to one's homeplace should be a tendency to look there for guides to thought and conduct. It appears from the data that Southerners *are* more likely to choose their "normative reference individuals" from among their neighbors and kin.[18]

On three of the surveys in hand, respondents were asked: "What man that you have heard or read about, living today in any part of the *world*, do you admire the *most*?" (The emphasis is as given in the original questionnaires.) Despite the evident attempt by the survey organization to elicit the names of public figures, something on the order of a quarter of the Southern respondents insisted on naming relatives, friends, or strictly local personalities (table 4-1). The three surveys are not directly comparable, since the categories for coding responses are inconsistent, but in each case the proportion of Southerners who gave "localistic" responses seems to be greater than the proportion of non-Southerners who did so. The codes on the second survey are most nearly ideal, and here Southerners were twice as likely (28% to 14%) to name kinfolk or other local figures.

Table 4-2 shows the responses when respondents were asked to name the *woman* they most admired. Regional differences are again consistent and are

Table 4-1
"What Man That You Have Heard or Read About, Living Today in Any Part of the World, Do You Admire the Most?"; Responses of Southerners and Non-Southerners, 1958, 1963, and 1965

Percentage Replying:	1958[a] South	1958[a] Non-South	1963[b,d] South	1963[b,d] Non-South	1965[c,d] South	1965[c,d] Non-South
Family	2%	2%	9%	4%	5%	5%
Other Local	17	12	19	10	27	13
Total of above[e]	19%	14%	28%	14%	32%	18%
(N)	(252)	(904)	(720)	(2242)	(608)	(1870)

[a]AIPO 608. Codes are "husband or father" and "miscellaneous—U.S."
[b]AIPO 681. Codes are "family" and "local."
[c]AIPO 721. Codes are "family, friend" and "miscellaneous."
[d]N's in this column are weighted. Raw are approximately one-half of these figures.
[e]"Don't know" responses excluded from percentage base.

Table 4-2
"What Woman That You Have Heard or Read About, Living Today in Any Part of the World, Do You Admire the Most?" Responses of Southerners and Non-Southerners, 1958, 1963, and 1965

Percentage Replying:	1958[a] South	1958[a] Non-South	1963[b,d] South	1963[b,d] Non-South	1965[c,d] South	1965[c,d] Non-South
Family	8%	4%	11%	4%	11%	6%
Other local	20	9	12	4	14	7
Total of above[e]	28%	13%	23%	8%	25%	13%
(N)	(150)	(720)	(697)	(2230)	(556)	(1757)

[a]AIPO 608. Codes are "wife or mother" and "miscellaneous—U.S."
[b]AIPO 681. Codes are "family" and "local."
[c]AIPO 721. Codes are "family, friend" and "miscellaneous."
[d]N's in this column are weighted. Raw are approximately one-half of these figures.
[e]"Don't know" responses excluded from percentage base.

roughly the same size as before. The largest difference is again on the survey where the coding categories are best.

"I Wish I Was in Dixie": Ideal Residence

Attachment to a place should also result in a reluctance to leave it.[a] Although census data show Southerners to be about as likely as any other Americans to

---

[a]This indicator and the one above correspond to two of the three used by Alvin W. Gouldner to measure the localism of college teachers, ("Cosmopolitans and Locals: Toward an Analysis of Latent Social Roles—I," *Administrative Science Quarterly*, 2 [1957-1958]: p. 290). It is difficult to see what analogue exists for his third measure, "commitment to specialized or professional skills," and I suspect its linkage to localism is more empirical than conceptual.

leave their home states and region, there is abundant qualitative evidence from every juke box that they are much more likely to complain about having left.[19] It has been argued that an unwillingness to move, translated into economic terms as immobility of labor, may have served to retard the South's economic development.[20] (As for other economically backward groups, explanation based on cultural traits has competed with economic and political explanations in terms of "colonialism."[21] This argument is irrelevant here, however.)

Americans have been asked several times where in the United States they would like to live, if they could live anywhere they wished. Table 4-3 shows responses to that question over a period of a quarter of a century. (Note that despite changes in sampling methods by the Gallup organization and great changes in the American scene, the data show a remarkable consistency over time.)

The evidence for Southern localism is not as clearcut as we might wish. Although a large (and increasing) proportion of Southerners express content with their present state, they are matched in this respect by residents of the Pacific states (and, lately, by those of the Mountain states). At the risk of offending some Southerners, it might be argued that the apparent exception of the Western states may be due to their being inherently more loveable than the Southern

Table 4-3
"If You Could Live Anywhere in the United States That You Wanted to, What State Would You Choose?" Percentage Choosing Present State of Residence, by Region, 1939, 1944, and 1963

	1939[a,d]	1944[b,d]	1963[c,d]
South	64%	65%	72%
(N)	(468)	(328)	(739)
New England	66%	56%	62%
(N)	(241)	(196)	(218)
Middle Atlantic	59%	58%	61%
(N)	(701)	(698)	(704)
East Central	53%	45%	54%
(N)	(527)	(557)	(493)
West Central	45%	59%	69%
(N)	(431)	(421)	(467)
Mountain	59%	64%	76%
(N)	(187)	(153)	(136)
Pacific	83%	79%	76%
(N)	(207)	(227)	(399)
All Non-South	58%	57%	65%
(N)	(2294)	(2252)	(2417)

[a]AIPO 63.

[b]AIPO 337.

[c]AIPO 723. N's in this column are weighted. Raw are approximately one-half of these figures.

[d]"Don't know" responses excluded from percentage base.

states: in 1939, for instance, only 10% of the non-Southern respondents chose Southern states (and most of those picked Florida), while 22% of the non-Westerners chose Western states. With this evidence, at least, Southerners' fondness for the South seems harder to explain than Westerners' affection for their states.

Similar results are found for attachment to *region*. When asked where they would go if they had to leave their present states, Southern respondents are more likely than Easterners and Midwesterners to name another state in the same region (table 4-4). Whether they are more likely to do so than Westerners depends on whether the Pacific and Mountain states are counted as one region or two. Here again, the Western states were more attractive to outsiders: 41% of non-Westerners named the West; 21% of non-Southerners named the South, more than half of these picking Florida (compared to 28% of the Southerners who named a Southern state).

When asked where they would like their sons to go to college, Southerners display a similarly high degree of local attachment (table 4-5). Although Southern institutions have done poorly in most objective assessments of quality (none was among the "leading universities" designated in a recent American Council on Education report), two-thirds of the Southern respondents to a 1950 poll would prefer that their sons be educated in the South, a degree of in-region choice surpassed only by New Englanders.[22] (If the Central states are counted as one region, their figure approaches that for the South. Midwestern schools, however, were chosen by 15% of non-Midwesterners, Eastern schools by 29% of non-Easterners, but Southern schools by only 3% of non-Southerners.)

Table 4-4
"If You Had to Move Away From [This State], To What State Would You Most Like to Go?"; Percent Choosing Region of Residence, by Region

	Percentage[a]	(N)
SOUTH	55	(151)
New England	35	(132)
Middle Atlantic	11	(362)
EAST	28	(494)
East Central	12	(307)
West Central	9	(194)
CENTRAL	19	(501)
Mountain	33	(51)
Pacific	33	(135)
WEST	59	(186)

Source: AIPO 454, 1950.

[a]"Don't know" responses excluded from percentage base.

Table 4-5

"If You Had a Son of College Age and He Could Enter Any College or University in the United States and You Had Enough Money to Send Him, to Which One Would You Most Want Him to Go?"; Percent Choosing an Institution in the Same Region, by Region

	Percentage[a]	(N)
SOUTH	67	(101)
New England	79	(123)
Middle Atlantic	54	(318)
EAST	81	(441)
East Central	52	(220)
West Central	38	(138)
CENTRAL	64	(358)
Mountain	11	(28)
Pacific	52	(120)
WEST	47	(148)

Source: AIPO 454, 1950.

[a]"Don't know" responses and those not allowing location of the school excluded from percentage base.

To summarize: Westerners have a high opinion of their states, New Englanders have a high opinion of their colleges, and these opinions are shared by people in other parts of the country. Southerners have a high opinion of their states *and* of their colleges, and their opinions are shared by almost nobody. It is fair to conclude, I think, that these opinions reflect a localistic orientation.

Effects of Standardization

It may be that Southern localism is merely a residual manifestation of a folk culture which will vanish when the South becomes as urban and industrial as the rest of the country. There is no way to be certain. We can, however, conduct a thought experiment: think of the Southern population as divided into groups differing in education, occupation, and urban or rural residence; then ask what proportion of Southerners would choose, for instance, to send their sons to school in the South, if these groups were present in the South in the same proportions as they are now in the non-South. The technique of "test-factor standardization" allows us to answer this question. (See the Methodological Appendix for a detailed description, with examples.)

Table 4-6 shows the effects of standardization on Southerners' tendency to choose a kinsman or other local figure as the person they "most admire." The

Table 4-6

Effects of Standardization on Regional Differences in Choosing Local "Most Admired" Man and Woman

Item	Percentage of Southerners Giving Response	Percentage Difference (South)−(Non-South)	
		Raw	Standardized
"Most admired" man is family or local (AIPO 681)	28%	+14	+ 9
"Most admired" woman is family or local (AIPO 681)	23%	+15	+12
"Most admired" man is family, friend, local, miscellaneous, etc.[a]	29%	+13	+11

[a]Pooled data from AIPO 608, 681, and 721. Code categories differ—see table 4-1, above.

first column of figures shows the proportion of Southerners giving the localistic response to each of the items. The second column shows the difference between this figure and the proportion of non-Southerners who named *their* relatives or neighbors. The third column shows the difference remaining after the Southern figure has been standardized. The codes are least ambiguous for AIPO 681, so the figures from that survey have been treated separately at the top of the table.

In each case, standardization moves the Southern figure closer to the national norm, but in none does even half of the regional difference seem to be due to regional variation in education, occupation, and rurality.

Pooling the three surveys on which this question was asked gives enough cases in each of the standardization groups so that their responses may be examined separately (although the partial non-equivalence of the codes is an unknown factor at work). This is done in table 4-7. Note first the low cross-group variation for non-Southerners; they are all, by this measure, fairly cosmopolitan. Southerners, on the other hand, show considerable differences from one group to another. There is, in other words, considerable statistical interaction between region and the control variables.

The table shows the data for those Southern groups which differ most from their non-Southern counterparts, and for those which differ least. The most "Southern" of Southerners, in this respect, are rural and small town people, and are either uneducated (not high school graduates) or employed in low-status occupations. Those groups least "Southern" are either urban or educated, high-status people. "Cosmopolitanism" in the South appears to be related to connection to the national system, either through education and job or through skilled

Table 4-7

Regional Differences in Choice of "Most Admired" Man, for Selected Standardization Groups, South and Non-South

Group[a]	South % Local	N	Non-South % Local	N	Percentage Difference
Rural, uneducated business, professional, and white collar	56	(77)	10	(52)	+46
Uneducated farm	43	(144)	11	(148)	+32
Rural, educated labor	40	(90)	13	(211)	+27
Educated farm	40	(40)	18	(139)	+22
Town, educated labor	38	(45)	17	(199)	+21
Town, uneducated unskilled labor	33	(43)	15	(202)	+18
Town, educated white collar	13	(38)	10	(84)	+ 4
Rural, educated business, professional, and white collar	19	(89)	16	(210)	+ 3
Urban, uneducated skilled labor	16	(73)	21	(190)	− 5
Urban, educated white collar	6	(54)	14	(361)	− 8

Source: Pooled data from AIPO 608, 681, and 721.

[a]All other groups differ by between 6 and 14 points. Median difference = 10; inter-quartile range of differences = 15.

labor in an urban setting. There are many exceptions to this generalization, however: business and professional people are conspicuously absent, as are educated skilled laborers.

These general patterns—the "Old South" groups most localistic, and the least localistic groups being among the "New South" types—determine that the standardization will reduce the overall regional differences, while the many exceptions and the net positive difference for most groups determine that much of the difference will remain after standardization.

Table 4-8 shows the effects of standardization on the regional differences in local attachment examined above. (The surveys for which standardization is not shown did not contain all the necessary control items.)

Table 4-8

Effects of Standardization on Regional Differences in Attachment to State and Region

Item	Percentage of Southerners Giving Response	Percentage Difference (South)–(All Non-South)	
		Raw	Standardized
"If you could live anywhere in the United States that you wanted to, what state would you choose?" (AIPO 723) (State of Residence)	72%	+ 7	+ 4
"If you had to move away from [this state], to what state would you most like to go?" (AIPO 454) (State in Same Region)[a]	55%	+21	+20
" . . . to which [college] would you most want [your son] to go?" (AIPO 454) (College in Region)[b]	67%	+11	0

[a]Non-Southern regions are Northeast, Central, and West.

[b]Non-Southern regions are New England, Middle Atlantic, East Central, West Central, Mountain, and Pacific.

Here again, standardization reduces the differences; but for two of the three items, substantial proportions of the initial difference remains. With standardization, Southerners *are* no more likely than other Americans to choose a college in their own region, although the critic might object that this is still not taking sufficient account of the generally low quality of those institutions.

Trend and Outlook: Persisting Localism

The results of the standardization give little basis for expecting Southern localism to vanish entirely as the South becomes more urban and industrialized, and its citizens better educated. The findings on preferred college may indicate that their localism will become less unqualified, but presumably if the present trends toward sectional equalization of education and income continue, Southern colleges and universities will also improve. It seems likely that Southerners will continue to prefer, other things equal, their local institutions: and increasingly, it appears, other things will be equal.

The actual trend data on choices of normative reference individuals are difficult to interpret, given the inconsistency of the codes. Since the categories used in 1963 were less inclusive than those used in 1958, we can say that Southerners were more likely at the later date to name a local figure as the man they most admired, although we can conclude nothing about the woman they admired most or about the responses of non-Southerners (tables 4-1 and 4-2). With the dubious assumption that the percent differences from the three surveys are directly comparable, we can say that the regional difference in localism, as measured by these responses, increased between 1958 and 1963, and remained roughly constant thereafter.

The trend data on preferred residence in table 4-3 show a slight increase between 1939 and 1963 in the proportion of Southerners choosing their own states, while all other regions except the West Central and Mountain states showed a decrease or no change in this period. Overall, there was no appreciable change in the *difference* between Southerners and non-Southerners during this twenty-four year period.

Southerners seem to have retained to a greater degree than other Americans a localistic orientation—an attachment to their place and their people. Although there are some cracks in this pattern, localism can be expected to color the outlook of many Southerners for some time to come.

5

"To Live — and Die — in Dixie": Southern Violence

"Southerners," someone once remarked, "will be polite until they're angry enough to kill you." He might have added that this flashpoint seems to be lower for Southerners than for other Americans. Beneath the image of a gracious, hospitable, leisurely folk has lurked that of a hot-tempered, violent, even sadistic people, an image "so pervasive that it compels the attention of anyone interested in understanding the South."[1]

Violence: Image and Reality

The Southern reputation for violence is one of long standing. The stereotype of the antebellum Southern gentleman was Mark Twain's Pembroke Howard, "a man always courteously ready to stand up before you in the field if any act or word of his had seemed doubtful or suspicious to you, and explain it with any weapon you might prefer from brad-awls to artillery." Although humorists and abolitionists undoubtedly exaggerated, force was of necessity a characteristic of slave society, and the image of the "lords of the lash" was not without foundation in fact. The duel *was* a frequent recourse of gentlemen (and, in its less elegant, eye-gouging variation, of non-gentlemen as well) long after it had, for all intents, disappeared elsewhere. Antebellum military men, practitioners of institutionalized violence, were disproportionately likely to be of Southern birth, and Southern statesmen took the lead in urging war throughout the early nineteenth century.[2] There seems to have been a peculiarly Southern disposition to use force to settle personal, sectional, and national grievances.[3] (It was, after all, a South Carolinian who caned Massachusetts' Charles Sumner on the Senate floor, not vice versa.)

After the war, violence was perhaps still more characteristic of Southern life.[4] Emancipation removed from Southern Negroes even the tenuous protection which their status as property had given, and in the conflict over what their "place" was to be, uncounted numbers were flogged and hundreds lynched. The emergence of lynching, elsewhere a frontier phenomenon, lends support to Cash's characterization of the Reconstruction South as "the frontier the Yankee made."[5] Lynching lasted well into the twentieth century, dying out only to be replaced by a rash of "civil-rights murders," the bombing of schools and churches, and miscellaneous violence by police and private citizens at the University of Mississippi, Birmingham, Selma, and elsewhere.

Nor has all of this violence been directed against Negroes. Among the victims of lynchers between 1889 and 1930 were 788 white men.[6] Although the formal duel was suppressed, a less ritualized form persisted in the rural South well into this century. (H. C. Brearley observed that a remark made in the 1890s was still valid in the 1930s: "It has been found impossible to convict men of murder . . . , provided the jury is convinced that the assailant's honor was aggrieved and that he gave his adversary notice of his intention to assail him.")[7,a] In the southern hills, great family feuds and the murderous exploits of moonshining outlaws helped to keep the image of Southern violence before the public. Meanwhile, beneath the more spectacular incidents, white Southerners have been doing away with one another privately at a prodigious rate. There are large and persistent differences between Southern and non-Southern whites in the frequency with which they actually murder people.[8]

Although a recent Harris Poll has shown that there are some situations in which Southerners are no more or even less likely to approve of violence than are non-Southerners, the historical record and the actual crime statistics suggest that Southerners do have a "tendency to appeal to force" to settle differences, and it may be supposed that they view such resort as more often legitimate than do non-Southerners.[9] If this is so, it is consistent with a number of diverse regional differences remarked by many observers, from the higher prestige of career military men in the South to Southern support for intervention in World War II.[10]

In this chapter, we shall examine regional differences in attitudes and behaviors of two sorts: those concerning private ownership and use of guns, and those concerning corporal punishment of children. As Hackney has observed, each might contribute to the maintenance of regional differences in homicide rates; at the very least they may be viewed as aspects of a more general acceptance of violence and the use of force.

"Below the Smith and Wesson Line"

Southerners are at least *potentially* more trigger-happy than other Americans: as table 5-1 shows, they are more likely to own guns. One possible explanation of higher Southern murder rates might run as follows: in a relatively rural population, where firearms are widely used for shooting vermin and for hunting, the

---

[a]This Southern understanding that a variety of circumstances require deadly retaliation probably explains the otherwise curious disinclination of Southerners to endorse, in the abstract, capital punishment for murder. There has been a persistent regional difference of ten or twelve percentage points in this respect for at least twenty-five years. See Hazel Erskine, "The Polls: Capital Punishment," *Public Opinion Quarterly* 34 (1970): 291. There definitely is not a general benevolence toward criminals in the South: Southerners are *more* likely to favor public whipping "or worse" for sex criminals (NORC 341/342, 1953) and to favor disfranchising convicts (AIPO 714; 1965).

availability of guns turns what would otherwise be shouting matches or fist-fights into shooting affrays. (Brearley observed, in support of this argument, that about three-quarters of Southern homicides in the 1930s were commited with firearms, compared with less than half of those in New England.[11]) But table 5-2, which presents data on hunting, indicates that regional differences in gun-ownership are larger than can be accounted for by this factor alone.[12] It is apparent that Southerners who do *not* hunt are more likely to own guns than non-hunters elsewhere. Even if the Southern murder rate is higher solely because of the availability of guns, we still have to inquire why there are so many guns lying around.

One possibility lies in the welter of state laws which deal with gun ownership. It is easier to own and use a gun legally in most Southern states. But this obser-

Table 5-1
Gun-ownership, by Region, 1959-1968

"Do you happen to have in your home any guns or revolvers?" (% "yes")	1959[a]	1965[b]	1968[c]
South	66%	62%	52%
(N)	(299)	(553)[d]	
Non-South	44%	46%	27%
(N)	(1074)	(2066)[d]	
Difference (South)–(Non-South)	22	16	25

Table 5-2
Hunting, by Region, 1959-1965

"Do you, or does your husband/ wife go hunting?" (% "yes")	1959[a]	1965[b]
South	53%	41%
(N)	(298)	(553)[d]
Non-South	33%	38%
(N)	(1070)	(2066)[d]
Difference (South)–(Non-South)	20	3

[a]AIPO 616.
[b]AIPO 704.
[c]Opinion Research, Inc., survey for CBS program of 2 September 1968, reported in Hackney, "Southern Violence," p. 919. Question-wording and sample sizes not reported.
[d]Weighted N. Raw is approximately one-half of this figure.

vation begs the question of why the people of the South have not, as table 5-3 shows, supported restrictions on gun ownership (and, in any event, homicide rates are not strikingly different in those Southern states which have strict controls).[13] Hackney has also pointed out that simple assault rates are higher in the South, indicating that Southern murders are not merely assaults which turned into murders due to the ease of access to guns.[14] It appears that Southerners are simply less uncomfortable with the implications and potentialities of what one state attorney general called "an armed camp in time of peace."[15]

"The Tune of a Hickory Stick"

Hackney has suggested that the Southern pattern of violence may be due to regional differences in child-rearing practices, hazarding a guess (in the absence of data) that Southerners are more likely to beat their children, who, when they grow up, are therefore more likely to be violent themselves.[16] He does not address the question of why Southerners are more likely to employ corporal punishment, but, if such punishment is going out of style, one explanation is simple cultural lag.

Table 5-4 shows that Southerners are more likely to report that they themselves were spanked as children and that they approve of spanking children. If we accept their reminiscences as an accurate report of childrearing practices when they were growing up and assume that those who do not approve of spanking children do not, in fact, spank their children, it appears that over the years before 1946 (when these data were collected) there had been a decline in the prevalence of corporal punishment in both South and non-South, consistent with a cultural lag explanation of the difference.

The data in table 5-5, however, do not support such an interpretation. Between 1946 and 1958, there was a marked *increase* in *both* regions in support for corporal punishment. The items ask specifically about the right of school officials to spank children, but, presumably, asserting that they have such a right indicates even more acceptance of corporal punishment than does the belief that parents should spank their own children. (On the one occasion when the two questions were asked on the same survey, nearly all respondents who approved of corporal punishment in the schools approved of it—or at least employed it—in their homes.)[17]

Respondents were also asked on three occasions if discipline was too severe or not severe enough in their schools, and Southerners were if anything *less* likely to say "not severe enough."[18] The greater acceptance by Southerners of corporal punishment in the schools then, seems not to represent a response to perceived disorder, but a peculiarly Southern acceptance of the use of force.

Southerners seem to be getting what they want from their schools. A poll of the readers of *Grade Teacher* magazine revealed that 70% of the Southern re-

Table 5-3

Opposition to Restrictions on Gun Ownership, South and Non-South, 1959-1965

	July 1959[b]	December 1963[c]	January 1965[d]	September 1965[e]
"Do you think it should be legal or illegal for private citizens to have loaded weapons in their homes?" (% "legal")[a]				
South	57%		70%	
(N)	(269)		(511)[f]	
Non-South	38%		44%	
(N)	(1004)		(1906)[f]	
Difference (South)–(Non-South)	19		26	
"What about the possession of pistols and revolvers— do you think there should be a law which would forbid the possession of this type of gun except by the police or other authorized persons?" (% "should not")[a]				
South	44%		63%	
(N)	(279)		(492)[f]	
Non-South	36%		43%	
(N)	(1016)		(1934)[f]	
Difference (South)–(Non-South)	8		20	
"Would you favor or oppose a law which would require a person to obtain a police permit before he or she could buy a gun?" (% "oppose")[a]				
South	31%	26%	36%	35%
(N)	(282)	(900)[f]	(525)[f]	(705)[f]
Non-South	20%	17%	22%	23%
(N)	(1044)	(2714)[f]	(1985)[f]	(2287)[f]
Difference (South)–(Non-South)	11	9	14	12

[a]"Don't know" responses excluded from percent base.
[b]AIPO 616.
[c]AIPO 681.
[d]AIPO 704.
[e]AIPO 717.
[f]Weighted N. Raw is approximately one-half this figure.

Table 5-4
Corporal Punishment in Own Childhood and Beliefs About Corporal Punishment, South and Non-South

	South	Non-South	Difference (South)–(Non-South)
"Were you spanked as a child?" (% "yes")	92%	83%	9
(N)	(395)	(2640)	
"Do you approve or disapprove of spanking children?" (% "approve")[a]	85%	72%	13
(N)	(383)	(2560)	

Source: AIPO 377, 1946.
[a]"Don't know" responses excluded from percentage base.

Table 5-5
Attitudes Toward Corporal Punishment in Schools, South and Non-South, 1938-1958

	1938[b]	1946[c]	1954[d]	1958[e]
% Who Approve Corporal Punishment in Schools[a]				
South	76%	59%	74%	81%
(N)	(458)	(380)	(385)	(301)
Non-South	50%	33%	48%	58%
(N)	(2255)	(2568)	(975)	(1046)
Difference (South)–(Non-South)	26	26	26	23

[a]"Don't know" responses excluded from percentage base.
[b]AIPO 114. "Do you think schoolteachers should be allowed to spank disobedient children at school?"
[c]AIPO 377. "Do you think teachers in grade school should have the right to spank children at school?"
[d]AIPO 538. "Do you think school officials should ever have the right to give pupils a licking?"
[e]AIPO 608. "Some teachers say they should have the right to punish students in grade school by paddling them. Do you think they should be allowed to do this, or not?"

spondents had used "physical punishment" in the last year, compared to 37% of the Easterners, 38% of the Westerners, and 54% of the Midwesterners.[19] Whether the use of force is a factor perpetuating the acceptance of force (as well as a manifestation of that acceptance) cannot be determined from the data (although, as Hackney observes, there are strong theoretical reasons for supposing so).[20]

Effects of Standardization

Simultaneous controls for education, occupation, and rurality produce here, as in the preceding chapter, only partial reduction of the demonstrated regional difference.[b] Table 5-6 shows the effects of standardization on gun ownership, hunting, and attitudes toward gun control. The largest reduction produced is in actual gun ownership, but the control variables explain less than half of the regional difference. For the item with the largest initial difference—opinion on

Table 5-6
Effects of Standardization on Regional Differences in Gun-related Attitudes and Behavior

Item	Percentage of Southerners Giving Response	Percentage Difference (South)–(Non-South) Raw	Standardized
"Do you happen to have in your home any guns or revolvers?"[a] ("yes")	63%	+14	+8
"Do you or does your husband/wife go hunting?"[a] ("yes")	45%	+9	+7
"Do you think it should be legal or illegal for private citizens to have loaded weapons in their homes?"[a] ("legal")	65%	+23	+23
" . . . do you think there should be a law [restricting handguns to] police or other authorized persons?"[a] ("no")	56%	+15	+11
"Would you favor or oppose a law which would require a person to obtain a police permit before he or she could buy a gun?"[b] ("oppose")	31%	+11	+9

[a]Pooled data from AIPO 616 and 704.
[b]Pooled data from AIPO 616, 681, 704, 717.

---

[b]For nearly all of the items examined in this chapter there are sex differences in response of about the same order of magnitude as the regional differences. Examination of the data showed, however, no appreciable regional differences in age or sex distribution, so it is not necessary to control for these variables.

On almost every item, sex differences were smaller in the South than in the non-South. With respect to violence, in other words, Southern women are less "feminine," both absolutely and relative to their men, than are non-Southern women.

whether citizens should be allowed to keep loaded guns in their homes—standardization makes no difference. On the other three items, standardization explains from about 20% to about 30% of the regional difference.

Table 5-7 reveals that there is very little interaction of region with the control variables. Most strata show regional differences of around 10%. There is no readily discernible pattern in those groups which differ by either much more or much less than this amount.

In table 5-8, standardization is seen to produce results comparable to those above. Reductions in the regional difference range from none, for reports on whether the respondent was spanked as a child, to somewhat under 25% of the original difference.

Table 5-9 shows the responses of different subgroups to the items on corporal punishment in the schools. Here, as above, there is little interaction between region and the control variables. Most groups in the South differ from the equiv-

Table 5-7

Proportion Who Oppose Requiring Police Permit for Purchase of a Gun, for Selected Standardization Groups, South and Non-South

Group[a]	South		Non-South		Difference (South)−(Non-South)
	%	N	%	N	
Rural, uneducated business, professional, white collar	37	(71)	15	(75)	+22
Town, uneducated skilled labor	44	(54)	26	(146)	+18
Urban, educated white collar	31	(121)	14	(541)	+17
Rural, educated labor	29	(129)	26	(339)	+ 2
Urban, uneducated unskilled labor	14	(88)	13	(565)	+ 1
Urban and town, uneducated white collar	12	(50)	12	(174)	0
Urban, uneducated skilled labor	17	(103)	18	(411)	− 1
Town, uneducated unskilled labor	20	(84)	32	(318)	−12

Source: Pooled data from AIPO 616, 681, 704, 717.

[a]All other standardization groups show regional differences of between 6 and 13 percent. Median difference = 9.5; inter-quartile range of differences = 7.

Table 5-8

Effects of Standardization on Regional Differences in Attitudes Toward Corporal Punishment

Item	Percentage of Southerners Giving Response	Percentage Difference (South)–(Non-South) Raw	Standardized
"Were you spanked as a child?" (AIPO 377, 1946) ("yes")	92%	+9	+9
"Do you approve or disapprove of spanking children?" (AIPO 377, 1946) ("approve")	85%	+12	+10
Approve corporal punishment in schools[a]	71%	+29	+22

[a]Pooled data from AIPO 377, 538, 608. For question-wordings, see table 5-5.

alent non-Southern groups by about 23%, with none departing from this pattern by much and no obvious pattern to those which depart from it more than others.

The effects of standardization, in general, then, are similar to those in the preceding chapter—that is, slight. Most of the original regional differences are reduced somewhat, but none is reduced by even a quarter. The differences, while in the direction of those produced by the South's lag in urbanization, industrialization, and education, are of sufficient magnitude that they cannot be accounted for by that lag alone. The absence of appreciable interaction between region and the control variables suggests that, with respect to violence, there may be a "Southern factor" which can almost be tacked on, additively, to a prediction based on education, occupation, and urban or rural residence.

Trend and Outlook: The South As Wave of the Future?

The results of the standardization indicate that one cannot rely on regional demographic convergence to obliterate the demonstrated regional differences in attitudes toward firearms and corporal punishment. To the extent that these attitudes contribute to or are indicative of a more general "subculture of violence"

Table 5-9

Proportion Who Favor Corporal Punishment in Schools, for Selected Standardization Groups, South and Non-South

| | South | | Non-South | | Difference |
Group[a]	%	N	%	N	(South)–(Non-South)
Urban, uneducated skilled labor	69	(28)	37	(260)	+32
Educated farmers and farm labor	80	(73)	50	(201)	+29
Town, educated white collar	71	(45)	43	(128)	+28
Rural, uneducated business, professional, white collar	83	(29)	66	(32)	+17
Urban, educated business and professional	52	(50)	35	(489)	+17
Rural, educated labor	81	(37)	64	(73)	+17
Urban, educated labor	52	(35)	37	(425)	+15
Rural, uneducated labor	89	(110)	75	(151)	+14

Source: Pooled data from AIPO 377, 538, 608.

[a]All other standardization groups show regional differences of between 20 and 26 percent. Median difference = 23; inter-quartile range of differences = 8.

in the South, that subculture cannot be expected to disappear. The trend data displayed above support the same conclusion.

Tables 5-1 and 5-2 do show a very substantial decrease in the regional difference in the proportion of hunters, without a corresponding decrease in the difference in the proportion of gun-owners. These two figures taken together, however, would seem to indicate that between 1959 and 1965 the proportion of non-hunters owning guns increased in the South and decreased elsewhere.

Table 5-3 shows, for every item but the last, an *increase* in the regional difference over time. Oddly enough, the non-South appears to be moving toward the Southern position, that is, it is getting more permissive about firearms, although the South is getting more permissive even faster—thus widening the gap. On the last item (whether a police permit should be required to own a gun) there is no consistent trend in the regional difference, although both regions may be becoming more permissive.[c]

[c]The second observation in this series was taken a month after President Kennedy's assassination. Note that the proportion permissive was temporarily reduced both in the South and elsewhere, but that it regained and exceeded its original level within little more than a year.

If the data reported in table 5-4 on corporal punishment when the respondents were children and their present feelings about corporal punishment are interpreted as trend data, they show an increasing regional difference in this respect. The actual trend data reported in table 5-5, on corporal punishment in the schools, show no substantial reduction of the regional difference between 1938 and 1958. Here again, the pattern after 1946 was one of the rest of the nation moving toward the Southern position, as the South became even more "Southern." The net result was no reduction of the regional difference.

It may appear that the South had, during the past generation, the dubious distinction of being in the vanguard of a national trend—it was the most violent region in an increasingly violent nation. Although there are indications that violence has been increasing in the United States, the connection between a general pattern of violence and data on gun control attitudes and childrearing practices is embarrassingly tenuous.[21] As indicators of a regional difference for which external documentation exists in abundance, the data are somewhat better, and their use in this analysis will rest at that.

6

"The Bible Belt":
Southern Religion

"Almost every observer of the South," according to Joseph Fichter and George Maddox, "has, sooner or later, recorded impressions about the pervasiveness and peculiarity of religious behavior and institutions in the region."[1] Some have been more sympathetic than others. H. L. Mencken, in one of his South-baiting moods, blasted the region as the "bunghole of the United States, a cesspool of Baptists, a miasma of Methodism, snake-charmers, phony real-estate operators, and syphilitic evangelists," while not a few Southerners have suspected that the South was and is the "last great bulwark of Christianity," "defender of the ark, its people . . . the Chosen People."[2] Although observers evaluate Southern religion differently, there has been general agreement about the ways in which it differs from that practiced in the rest of the United States (or, for that matter, in the rest of the world). Let us examine some of these differences.

"Baptist-Methodist Hegemony"

Probably the most striking feature of religion in the South is that the region is, and has been since antebellum times, monolithically Protestant. Richard Weaver remarked that "a religious solid South preceded the political solid South," and the first will apparently outlast the latter as well.[3] Table 6-1 summarizes the data on religious identity from twenty-eight AIPO surveys conducted between 1954 and 1966. Nine out of ten Southerners identified themselves as Protestant in this period, compared to only six of every ten non-Southerners. While these proportions varied slightly from survey to survey, pooling the data gives sufficiently large bases to inspire considerable confidence in the aggregate estimate.[a]

Not only is the South more uniformly Protestant than the rest of the country, its Protestant population is itself more homogeneous—and in a way that makes the region unique. A geographer, Wilbur Zelinsky, has identified the South as one of seven "religious regions" in the United States, on the basis of Baptist dominance and Methodist strength, and Samuel S. Hill, Jr., has noted that "at no other time and place in the history of Christianity have low-church

---

[a]The diversity of the rest of the country is somewhat exaggerated by the aggregate figure, since the "non-South" is composed of several regions, each of which *might* be totally homogeneous. However, Hill, in *Southern Churches in Crisis*, makes it quite clear that "the Protestant hegemony in Dixie is unparalleled elsewhere" (pp. 31-39; quote from p. 34). He excludes only "the Mormon domain" from his conclusion.

Table 6-1

"What is Your Religious Preference—Protestant, Catholic, or Jewish?": Proportion Protestant, South and Non-South, 1954-1966

Years	1954-1959[a]	1961-1963[b]	1964-1966[c]
Pooled Data			
% Protestant, South	90%	88%	87%
(N)	(2930)	(7195)[d]	(6960)[d]
% Protestant, Other	60%	62%	58%
(N)	(9582)	(23237)[d]	(20905)[d]
Separate Studies			
South			
Median % Protestant	89%	88%	88%
Range, % Protestant	83-96%	86-94%	82-91%
Range, (N)	(197-397)	(566-964)[d]	(553-891)[d]
Other			
Median, % Protestant	58%	62%	59%
Range, % Protestant	54-68%	58-65%	54-63%
Range, (N)	(840-1175)	(1831-2835)[d]	(2066-2471)[d]
No. of Studies	9	10	9

[a]Pooled data from AIPO 531, 538, 543, 555, 580, 604, 607, 608, 616. NORC 294 (1950), 341 (1953), and 404 (1957) give figures within the range established by the AIPO studies, but have not been included, since the question-wordings are not strictly comparable.
[b]Pooled data from AIPO 642, 648, 649, 651, 652, 660, 662, 670, 676, 681.
[c]Pooled data from AIPO 686, 702, 704, 710, 714, 717, 718, 721, 723.
[d]Weighted N's. Raw are approximately half of these.

Protestant groups achieved majority status and the chief position of responsibility."[4] Table 6-2 pools data from four surveys which asked for the denominational affiliation of Protestant respondents. Nearly half of the Southern Protestants are Baptist, roughly three times the relative frequency of this denomination outside the South. (To compound the regional difference, the bulk of the South's Baptists are affiliated with the Southern Baptist Convention: they are, one might say, *ultra* Baptists.)[5] Methodists and Presbyterians make up about the same proportions of the Southern Protestant population as of the non-Southern Protestant population. Together, these three denominations account for all but about one in five Southern Protestants and nearly three-quarters of all Southerners. Fewer than half of the non-Southern Protestants, and fewer than one in three non-Southerners generally, identify themselves with one of these denominations.

If anything, the religious homogeneity of most Southern communities is understated by these data, since Southerners not in the religious mainstream are

Table 6-2
Denominational Composition of Protestants, South and Non-South, 1950-1965

1950-1955[a]	South	Non-South
Baptist	49%	17%
Methodist	24	24
Presbyterian	6	10
Other	22	50
TOTAL	101%[c]	101%[c]
(N)	(599)	(1110)
1962-1965[b]	South	Non-South
Baptist	48%	13%
Methodist	21	21
Presbyterian	10	10
Other	21	56
TOTAL	100%	100%
(N)	(1386)[d]	(2815)[d]

[a]Pooled data from AIPO 543 ("What is your denomination?"); NORC 294 ("What denomination?"). Definition of "South" slightly different on latter; see Methodological Appendix.
[b]Pooled data from AIPO 660, 710 ("What Protestant denomination–Baptist, Methodist, Lutheran, Presbyterian, or what?").
[c]Total differs from 100% due to rounding error.
[d]Weighted N. Raw is approximately one-half of this.

geographically concentrated *within* the South.[6] Hero reports that three of the ten locales he studied contained no known non-Protestants.[7]

The truth of the dictum laid down by Fichter and Maddox—that "religion in the South has been largely a Protestant affair"—virtually requires that this inquiry be restricted to Protestants.[8] Attempts to control for religion would be largely futile, due to the small number of non-Protestant Southerners responding to each survey. Consequently, in most of the following tables, regional comparisons have been made for Protestants only, to avoid confounding regional differences with "the religious factor."[9] Occasionally, Catholics (not divided by region) will be included as a comparison group.

The Articles of Southern Faith

The Old South's attitude toward religion, Richard Weaver observed, was "essentially the attitude of orthodoxy; . . . the simple acceptance of a body of belief."[10] Seventy years after Appomattox, another scholar could remark of the South that "heresy is still heresy with the vast majority of people."[11] Two generations later still, that old-time religion seems to remain good enough for nearly all Southern Protestants.

The orthodox consensus in the South is striking and consistent. Table 6-3 shows the responses to several questions about Christian beliefs. On every one of eight comparisons, from four AIPO surveys, a higher proportion of Southerners than of non-Southerners indicated belief, and the regional differences among Protestants are frequently greater than Protestant-Catholic differences. (Differ-

Table 6-3
Religious Beliefs of Southern Protestants, Non-Southern Protestants, and Catholics[a]

| | Protestants | | |
	South	Non-South	Catholics
"Do you, personally, believe in God?" (% "yes")[b]	98% (251)	98% (1160)	98% (504)
"Do you, yourself, believe in God?" (% "yes")[c]	99% (271)	99% (620)	99% (309)
"Do you believe that Jesus Christ was the Son of God or just a man?" (% "Son of God")[d]	99% (303)	90% (678)	95% (367)
"Do you, yourself, believe there is a God who is aware of the things we do in our daily life?" (% "yes")[b]	97% (250)	88% (1157)	93% (500)
"Please tell me in your own words, what you believe about life after death." (% giving response indicating belief)[b]	82% (256)	76% (1172)	89% (514)
"Do you believe there is or is not life after death?" (% "believe there is")[d]	89% (301)	75% (679)	71% (370)
"Do you believe that there is or is not a devil?" (% "believe there is")[d]	86% (301)	52% (676)	65% (368)
"Do you think Jesus Christ will ever return to earth?" (% "yes")[e]	81% (267)	56% (629)	46% (357)

[a]"Don't know" responses included in percentage base.
[b]AIPO 407, 1947.
[c]AIPO 539, 1954.
[d]AIPO 580, 1957.
[e]AIPO 622, 1959.

ences on the first two items are obscured by rounding, but were present.) On none of the items did the proportion of Southerners indicating unbelief (or even agnosticism) exceed 20%, a level of skepticism surpassed by non-Southern Protestants for half of the items, including those about life after death. Barely half of the non-Southerners believe in the devil, while Episcopal Bishop Robert Raymond Brown's observation that "The people [of the Deep South] believe strongly in an anthropomorphic Satan" is correct, if his impression that "they believe more in the reality of Satan than in the reality of God" is not.[12] In general, as the doctrines move further away from the bare minimum required to consider oneself religious at all, the proportion of non-Southerners subscribing drops off sharply, while, as it were, the "belief curve" of Southern Protestants is relatively inelastic.

The concrete, literal nature of Southern belief can be illustrated by comparison of two items in table 6-3. While Southern and non-Southern Protestants are about equally likely (nearly certain) to believe in God, the Southerners are much more likely to believe in a God Whose Eye is on the sparrow, or at least on them as they go about their day-to-day business. Similarly, examination of the detailed responses to the open-ended question about life after death reveals that Southerners were more likely to mention specific details such as Heaven, Hell, judgment, and bodily resurrection, and Northerners to speak more abstractly of "life everlasting," "eternal rest," or "peace."[13]

A distinction should be made, however, between orthodoxy and credulity. Poteat remarked thirty years ago on the lack of success in the South of the theologically unorthodox denominations of Unitarianism and Christian Science (to which could be added Mormonism and Spiritualism, at least), and Simkins has observed that "Southerners of neither race are lured away from the straight and narrow path by such heresies as those of Father Divine."[14] Southerners stick pretty close to Scripture: when asked if it is possible to communicate with the dead, they were *less* likely than non-Southerners to indicate belief (3% vs. 5%), despite the fact that they are more likely to believe in life after death in the first place.[15]

Given the extent of literal belief among Southern Protestants, it is perhaps not surprising that as many as 42% are convinced that a person cannot be a good Christian without literal belief in the New Testament. This is markedly higher than the proportion of non-Southern Protestants (19%) or that of Catholics (17%) subscribing to this opinion.[16]

The One True Churches: Sectarianism and
Religious Xenophobia

The extent of orthodoxy in the South is such that it virtually *must* cut across denominational lines, as many observers have claimed it does. Thus, Hill speaks of "a trans-denominational 'southern church,' embracing what may be called 'popular southern Protestantism.' " "This general tradition," he says, " 'what every schoolboy knows,' is the heart of the southern church's ideology. Catch almost any Southerner offguard, ask him what Christianity teaches, and he will produce the standard answer, a simple list of propositions to which the masses of churchmen almost unconsciously revert. . . . "[17] Or, as Poteat observed some time ago: " . . . the theology of the South is the same in its broad essentials among all the religious groups. . . . Scratch any sectarian skin and the same orthodox blood flows."[18]

Even if, as Francis Butler Simkins claimed, the proper simile for Southern denominationalism is not the Tower of Babel, but Joseph's coat of many colors ("a flawless ensemble"), the fact remains that Southern churches still permit themselves the occasional luxury of sectarian in-fighting.[19] Although sectarianism has been somewhat muted since the antebellum days when it "often influenced such important decisions as to whether a Methodist should marry a Baptist, or whether to vote for a staunch Baptist or an Episcopalian," the major Protestant denominations are still jealous of the distinctions which do exist.[20] Simkins declared it "no longer good manners, in pulpit or parlor, to criticize a church other than one's own," but went on to observe that

Southerners adhere firmly to the Christian dogma that there is but a single road by which a person can be saved. Because each denomination believes that it has the right road to the Heavenly Kingdom, there is no room for compromise with those who claim other roads.[21]

The nature of the accommodation which the more established Southern churches have reached with one another reinforces these divisive tendencies, but, at the same time, removes much of the element of competition. In the South, as elsewhere, each denomination (and, within denominations, each congregation) ministers primarily to a particular social stratum.[22] The picture is one of homogeneity within homogeneity. Although Pentecostal and Episcopalian may have the same creed, neither desires to worship with the other.

One indication of the importance of denominational distinctions to Southerners is their frequently remarked unresponsiveness to ecumenical overtures.[23] Table 6-4 shows a substantial—and increasing—majority of Southern Protestants opposed to the merger of all Protestant churches. Another indication may be the somewhat greater tendency of Southern Protestants to remain in the denomination in which they were raised (table 6-5).

This aloofness toward Protestants of denominations other than one's own may place the notorious Southern antipathy for non-Protestants in a somewhat different light. While the present data do not allow further examination of the problem, it seems likely that Southern anti-Semitism and anti-Catholicism have stronger components of religious hostility and relatively less of cultural nativism than the non-Southern varieties, especially given the protective cultural colora-

Table 6-4

"A Committee of Church People in the U.S. is Studying a Plan Whereby All Protestant Churches in This Country Would Join to Form a Single Protestant Church. What is Your Feeling About an Idea of This Kind—Would You Be in Favor of It or Opposed to It?" Responses of Southern Protestants and Non-Southern Protestants, 1950 and 1961

| | Percentage opposed to merger[a] | |
	1950[b]	1961[c]
Southern Protestants	61%	70%
(N)	(135)	(777)[d]
Non-Southern Protestants	39%	64%
(N)	(760)	(1505)[d]

[a]"Don't know" responses, on the order of 5-10% for both regions at both times, have been excluded from percentage base.
[b]AIPO 454.
[c]AIPO 642.
[d]Weighted N. Raw is approximately one-half this figure.

tion of many Southern Catholics and Jews.[24] Table 6-6 shows that these antipathies persist. Note that the least tolerated religious minority (especially in the South, where 42% of the Protestants would deny them the vote) is *atheists*, who are even less like Protestants, theologically, than are Catholics and Jews.[b]

Religiosity and Observance

This indelicate emphasis on religious differences may simply reflect the relative importance of religion for Southerners. Many have remarked the importance in the South of membership in a church and participation in its activities.[25] Simkins, for instance, claims that the South

forces religious conformity in a subtle and effective way, irritating the [visitor] by asking, "To what church do you belong?" If the answer is "No church what-

---

[b]This relatively high level of ideological or, one might say, "theoretical" anti-Semitism and anti-Catholicism coexists paradoxically with what seems to be a lower level of day-to-day discrimination and hostility. This may be due to lower visibility (the Southern assumption being that everyone is Protestant), or to a tradition of good manners in secondary interaction. In any event, it parallels an anomaly which bemused Hill, in "An Agenda for Research on Religion," p. 210: "Finally, is any differentiation to be made between Southern churchmen's attitudes toward other denominations as representations of Christianity, on the one hand, and their feelings toward persons in those other denominations, on the other? . . . [T]here seems to be no correlation between dogmatism [on the legitimacy of other denominations] and interpersonal relations in the Southern society."

Table 6-5
Apostasy Rates for Protestant Denominations, South and Non-South

		Percentage Formerly_ _ _ _ No Longer So[a]		
	Baptist	Methodist	Presbyterian	Church of Christ, Congregational
South	12%	15%	21%	28%
(N)	(188)	(78)	(14)	(18)
Non-South	18%	20%	34%	42%
(N)	(114)	(118)	(50)	(19)

Source: AIPO 543, 1955.

[a]From questions: "What is your denomination?"; "Has that always been your religious preference or affiliation?"; "What was your religious preference previously?" Bases too small for computation of stable percentages for other denominations.

Table 6-6
Attitudes Toward Religious Out-groups, of Southerners and Non-Southerners, 1958-1965

ATHEISTS

"If your party nominated a generally well-qualified man for President and he happened to be [an atheist], would you vote for him?"[b]

	Percentage saying "no"[a]	(N)
Southerners	92	(178)
Non-Southerners	77	(909)

"Do you think _____ should be permitted to vote, or not? . . . How about atheists, that is, those that don't believe in God?"[e]

	Percentage saying "should not"[a]	(N)
Southerners	42	(718)[h]
Non-Southerners	22	(2123)[h]

JEWS (Responses of Protestants and Catholics Only)

"If your party nominated a generally well-qualified man for President and he happened to be a [Jew], would you vote for him?"

		Percentage saying "no"[a]		
	1958[b]	1961[c]	1963[d]	1965[e]
Southerners	51%	51%	36%	30%
(N)	(166)	(509)[h]	(465)[h]	(707)[h]
Non-Southerners	28%	21%	13%	13%
(N)	(809)	(1920)[h]	(2051)[h]	(1993)[h]

Table 6-6 (cont.)

"And how would you feel about marrying a Jew? Which one of the statements . . . comes closest to your own feelings?"[f]

	Percentage saying "definitely would not"[a]	(N)
Southerners	70	(272)
Non-Southerners	55	(772)

"Would you have a serious objection to a daughter or son of yours marrying a Jew?"[g]

	Percentage saying "yes"[a]	(N)
Southerners	64	(288)
Non-Southerners	47	(936)

CATHOLICS (Responses of Protestants Only)

"If your party nominated a generally well-qualified man for President and he happened to be a [Catholic], would you vote for him?"

	Percentage saying "no"[a]			
	1958[b]	1961[c]	1963[d]	1965[e]
Southerners	50%	37%	38%	28%
(N)	(161)	(583)[h]	(418)[h]	(651)[h]
Non-Southerners	36%	13%	16%	10%
(N)	(515)	(1351)[h]	(1368)[h]	(1300)[h]

"Would you have a serious objection to a daughter or son of yours marrying a Catholic?"[g]

	Percentage saying "yes"[a]	(N)
Southerners	54	(281)
Non-Southerners	40	(668)

[a]"Don't know" responses excluded from percentage base.
[b]AIPO 604, 1958.
[c]AIPO 649, 1961.
[d]AIPO 676, 1963.
[e]AIPO 714, 1965.
[f]NORC 294, 1950.
[g]AIPO 608, 1958.
[h]Weighted N. Raw is approximately one-half of this.

ever," the Southerner turns away bewildered. Unless he is widely read or widely traveled, he can scarcely conceive of a person who is decent in dress, manners, and morals who has no church inclinations.[26]

Even allowing for exaggeration, it is apparent that Simkins is pointing to a regional distinction of some importance.

The present data show, in table 6-7, that a relatively large proportion of Southern Protestants believe that regular church attendance is prerequisite for being a good Christian. (In the later survey, they were more likely to believe this than Catholics, for whom attendance is a matter of formal obligation.)

This belief is coordinate with the greater likelihood of Southern Protestants to report that they attend church themselves "once a week or more" or "regularly" (table 6-8), or, perhaps a more valid measure, that they had been to church in the last week (table 6-9). (The figures in table 6-9 are subject to seasonal fluctuation, but there may be evidence of decreasing attendance both in the South and elsewhere.[27] Leaving aside the very first observation, however, there is only slight evidence of any diminution of regional *differences*.) Table 6-10 indicates that, in this respect at least, the regional differences hold up within denominations.

Southerners are not only more likely to attend church, they are more likely to "attend" worship services on radio or television.[28] Forty-five percent of all Southerners report listening "regularly" to religious services, compared to 30% of non-Southerners.[29] This may be due in part to the relative availability of such

Table 6-7

Beliefs Concerning Importance of Church-going, for Southern Protestants, Non-Southern Protestants, and Catholics, 1957 and 1963

	Percentage Saying One Cannot Be a Christian without Going to Church[a]		
	Southern Protestants	Non-Southern Protestants	Catholics
1957[b]	21%	12%	22%
(N)	(301)	(677)	(368)
1963[c]	36%	20%	28%
(N)	(821)[d]	(1732)[d]	(936)[d]

[a]"Don't know" responses included in percentage base.

[b]AIPO 580 ("Do you think a person can be a Christian if he doesn't go to church?").

[c]AIPO 681 ("Do you think a person can be a *good* Christian if he doesn't go to church?" Emphasis added. Note difference in wording from AIPO 580.)

[d]Weighted N. Raw is approximately one-half of this.

67

Table 6-8
Reported Church Attendance, for Southern and Non-Southern Protestants

1950[a] Attend Church:	Once a Week or More	Never	(N)
Southern Protestants	42%	12	(219)
Non-Southern Protestants	24%	22	(462)

1963[b] Attend Church:	Regularly	Seldom, Never	(N)
Southern Protestants	48%	20	(820)[c]
Non-Southern Protestants	41%	28	(1732)[c]

[a]NORC 294 ("About how often do you go to church or religious services?").

[b]AIPO 681 (From questions: ". . . do you attend church or religious services?"; "About how often do you go? Would you say you go *regularly, occasionally,* or *seldom*?").

[c]Weighted N. Raw is approximately one-half of this.

Table 6-9
"Did You, Yourself, Happen to Attend Church in the Last Seven Days?": Responses of Southern and Non-Southern Protestants, 1955-1964

| | Percentage Saying "Yes" | | |
Date[a]	Southern Protestants	Non-Southern Protestants	Difference
February 1955	55%	32%	+23
March 1957	52%	41%	+11
December 1958	51%	37%	+14
July 1959	43%	34%	+ 9
March 1961	49%	39%	+10
October 1961	45%	36%	+ 9
June 1962	45%	34%	+11
April 1963	46%	38%	+ 8
August 1963	41%	32%	+ 9
December 1963	46%	38%	+ 8
February 1964	46%	34%	+12
Range, (N)	(263-apx. 400)[b]	(610-apx. 850)[b]	

[a]AIPO 543, 580, 608, 616, 642, 651, 660, 670, 676, 681, 686.

[b]Maximum given is approximately one-half of highest weighted N.

programs, but it is a complete reversal of the usual pattern of media exposure: in 1950, for instance, 54% of Southerners and 68% of non-Southerners reported listening to radio *newscasts* more than fifteen minutes a day.[30]

The worship in which Southerners participate appears to be qualitatively different as well. The relative emotionalism of Southern religion has been remarked

Table 6-10

Differences in Church Attendance Between Southerners and Non-Southerners, within Denominations

Denomination:	Baptist		Methodist		Presbyterian and Episcopalian	
Region:	South	Other	South	Other	South	Other
Attend church once a week or more (1950)[a]	43%	31%	42%	19%	37%	24%
Never	13	27	13	23	7	26
(N)	(110)	(78)	(53)	(137)	(27)	(97)
Attended church last week (Feb. 1955)[b]	56%	29%	58%	26%	58%	31%
(N)	(181)	(106)	(88)	(123)	(26)	(101)
Attended church last week (June 1962)[c]	44%	27%	46%	29%	44%	34%
(N)	(301)[d]	(142)[d]	(173)[d]	(316)[d]	(75)[d]	(197)[d]

[a]NORC 294. See table 6-8 for question-wording.
[b]AIPO 543. See table 6-9 for question-wording.
[c]AIPO 660. See table 6-9 for question-wording.
[d]Weighted N. Raw is approximately one-half of this.

by many observers, and it is not restricted to Pentecostal snake-handlers in the backwoods.[31] Although some writers claim to see a decline in the emotional emphasis, Southerners are twice as likely as non-Southerners to report that they have had a "moment of sudden religious insight or awakening" (37% of Southern Protestants; 19% of non-Southern Protestants).[32]

The apparent greater salience of religion for Southerners is revealed in many ways. When asked on two occasions to name the man they most admired, Southerners were much more likely to name a religious leader (Billy Graham—13% on the first survey and 12% on the second, compared to 2% and 4% for non-Southerners).[33] This is a striking difference, even when allowance is made for the greater proportion of non-Protestants outside the South. (On the first of these surveys, evangelist and faith-healer Oral Roberts was named by another 2% of the Southern respondents.)

One discordant note is introduced by the data in table 6-11, which show Southern Protestants no more likely than their coreligionists in the North (and considerably *less* likely than Catholics) to pray regularly. There may be simply a regional difference in the definition of "regular" prayer, or—if the question was taken to refer to *private* prayer—regional differences in religious activity may be peculiar to its public and communal forms.

Table 6-11
Frequency of Prayer, for Southern Protestants, Non-Southern Protestants, and Catholics

Pray[a]	Protestants South	Non-South	Catholics
Regularly	62%	61%	76%
Seldom or Never	10	10	3
(N)	(820)[b]	(1732)[b]	(935)[b]

Source: AIPO 681, 1963.
[a]From questions: "Do you ever pray?"; "About how often—*frequently, occasionally*, or *seldom?*"
[b]Weighted N. Raw is approximately one-half of this.

Private Morality: The "Thou Shalt Nots"

Another characteristic of the Southern religion is its hard line on private morality, an "anti-fun, highly individualistic moral orientation," an emphasis on "the 'Thou shalt nots' of moral restriction."[34] Whatever behavior may actually be, the approved morality in the South is an austere one, with peculiar regional emphases.[35]

Table 6-12 presents a smattering of data on various aspects of what, despite the "Cavalier legend," must be called puritanism. Note in particular the large regional differences in attitudes and behaviors concerned with alcohol. Other studies have documented this difference, and many observers have commented on the Southern "eleventh commandment."[36]

Oddly, in the light of these data, Southern Protestants are nearly twice as likely as non-Southern Protestants (20% to 11%) to report that liquor has been "a cause of trouble" in their families. There is some evidence that Southerners who do drink (particularly women) may drink to excess, but it seems likely that the mere fact of drinking itself may be defined as a problem in the South.[37] It is one of the pleasant anomalies of American life that the region most chary of "cigarettes and whiskey and wild, wild women" (as the hillbilly song has it) produces nearly all of the first and the best of the second. (As for the last, reliable data are lacking. Kinsey et al. caution that their conclusions are least applicable to "groups originating in the Southeastern quarter of the country," due to relatively few cases.)[38]

Data not presented here show that Southerners may also be a bit less likely to approve the chewing of bubblegum.[39]

Public Morality: The Church Inert

The churches of the South have been much criticized of late for their inaction on pressing issues of public policy—notably racial desegregation. Were it not for

Table 6-12

Regional Differences in Selected Manners and Morals (Protestants Only)

"Do you ever have occasion to use alcoholic beverages such as liquor, wine, or beer—or are you a total abstainer?"[a]

	Percentage Abstain		
	1955[b]	1957[c]	1966[d]
Southerners	65%	67%	68%
(N)	(353)	(303)	(614)[j]
Non-Southerners	38%	39%	32%
(N)	(610)	(680)	(1388)[j]

"Would you favor or oppose a law forbidding the sale of all beer, wine and liquor throughout the nation?"

	Percentage Favor[e]	
	1957[c]	1966[d]
Southerners	56%	44%
(N)	(289)	(579)[j]
Non-Southerners	25%	20%
(N)	(644)	(1357)[j]

"Do you object to women drinking in public places such as bars and restaurants, or not?"[c,k]

	Percentage Oppose[g]
Southerners	74%
(N)	(296)
Non-Southerners	49%
(N)	(670)

"Do you approve or disapprove of women wearing shorts in public?"[f,k]

	Percentage Disapprove[e]
Southerners	84%
(N)	(622)[j]
Non-Southerners	68%
(N)	(1517)[j]

"If your party nominated a generally well-qualified man for President and he happened to be [divorced], would you vote for him?"

	Percentage Who Would Not[e]	
	1963[h]	1965[i]
Southerners	15%	20%
(N)	(415)[j]	(667)[j]
Non-Southerners	14%	11%
(N)	(1366)[j]	(1307)[j]

Table 6-12 (cont.)

---

aThere were minor variations in question-wording on the three surveys reported here.
bAIPO 543, 1955.
cAIPO 580, 1957.
dAIPO 723, 1966.
e"Don't know" responses excluded from percentage base.
fAIPO 651, 1961.
g"Don't know" responses included in percentage base.
hAIPO 676, 1963.
iAIPO 714, 1965.
jWeighted N. Raw is approximately one-half this figure.
kTables not presented here show no interaction of region and sex.

the historical record, one could be pardoned for supposing that there is a peculiarly Southern tendency to keep the church "above politics." The vigorous efforts of the Southern church in defense of slavery, in the fight for Prohibition, against the teaching of evolutionary theory, and in the election of 1928, however, should raise some doubts about just how apolitical the Southern church really is.[40] The data in table 6-13 give little support to such a notion, either.

Yet, despite impressive pronouncements on the immorality of racial segregation by nearly all denominations at the regional level, the situation at the local level is such that Fichter and Maddox can observe: "it may be said without disrespect that the churches seem to employ God to maintain and retain the Old South."[41] (Ralph McGill, less respectfully, charged that white supremacists "employ God and Christ somewhat as cosmic bellboys."[12]) Why should there be, on this issue, such a great gulf fixed between the Church and the churches? Part of the story, no doubt, lies in the attitudes of local clergymen, many of whom are Southerners and who may share their parishioners' views to some extent.[43] But there is more to it than that.

The explanation can be approached either subtly by analysis of the patterns

Table 6-13
"Should the Churches Keep Out of Political Matters or Should They Express Their Views on Day-to-Day Social and Political Questions?" Responses of Southern Protestants, Non-Southern Protestants, and Catholics

	Percentage saying churches should keep out of politics[a]	(N)
Southern Protestants	44%	(298)
Non-Southern Protestants	47%	(670)
Catholics	45%	(368)

Source: AIPO 580, 1957.
a"Don't know" responses included in percentage base.

of lay control in the region's relatively non-hierarchical dominant churches, or graphically with case histories of clergymen harried from the pulpit for integrationist sentiments.[44] Not to belabor the point, it appears that most Southern churches are potentially by structure and actually, given the high level of involvement documented above, so much a part of the community as to be indistinguishable from it, leading to a situation where, as Manschreck put it: "Religion is saying no more to society than society is saying to itself."[45] Thus, Jehovah becomes "a tribal god," and scripture is quoted to support causes and institutions which may appear to the non-Southerner as irrelevant to or inconsistent with his understanding of Christianity.[46]

It is not surprising, perhaps, if Southerners perceive religion as sanctioning Southern institutions which are manifestly in decline, that they are more likely than non-Southerners to feel that religion's influence on American life is decreasing (table 6-14). They certainly do not attribute the decreasing influence to

Table 6-14
"At the Present Time, Do You Think Religion as a Whole Is Increasing Its Influence on American Life or Losing Its Influence?" Responses of Southern Protestants, Non-Southern Protestants, and Catholics

	Percentage saying "losing"[a]	(N)
Southern Protestants	21%	(274)
Non-Southern Protestants	12%	(644)
Catholics	7%	(356)

Source: AIPO 580, 1957.
[a]Other responses were "increasing," "same," and "don't know."

Table 6-15
Proportions of Southerners and Non-Southerners Indicating the Most Important Problem Facing U.S. is "Loss of Religion"; 1950, 1962, and 1965

	1950[a]	1962[b]	1965[c]	1965[d]
Southerners	5%	2%	1%	4%
(N)	(168)	(775)[e]	(799)[e]	(752)[e]
Non-Southerners	1%	1%	1%	—%
(N)	(1236)	(2320)[e]	(2290)[e]	(2382)[e]

[a]AIPO 454 ("What do you think is the most important problem facing the entire country today?"—code: "religious problems, need churches").
[b]AIPO 662 ("What do you think is the most important problem facing this country today?"—code: "Religious problems; the need for more faith in God, Religion, etc.")
[c]AIPO 714 ("What do you think is the most important problem facing this country today?"—code: "Religion [lack of]").
[d]AIPO 717 (same question-wording and code as AIPO 714).
[e]Weighted N. Raw is approximately one-half this figure.

shortcomings of religion itself. Table 6-16 reveals that nearly all believe that religion can answer today's problems, and they are *more* likely to believe this than Catholics or non-Southern Protestants. Nor do they attribute religion's declining influence to its organizational form. Table 6-17 confirms Hill's observation that Southern churches have a "very special self-estimate." (They "not infrequently . . . boast of their success in conforming to the New Testament ideal."[47]) When asked what changes they would like to see in their churches, more than half of the Southern Protestants volunteered that no change was needed (52%, compared to 49% of non-Southern Protestants—the regional difference is much larger among the dominant Baptists and Methodists), although "no change

Table 6-16
"Do You Believe That Religion Can Answer All or Most of Today's Problems, or Is It Largely Old-Fashioned and Out-of-Date?" Responses of Southern Protestants, Non-Southern Protestants, and Catholics

	Percentage saying religion can answer today's problems[a]	(N)
Southern Protestants	90%	(299)
Non-Southern Protestants	81%	(674)
Catholics	82%	(368)

Source: AIPO 580, 1957.
[a]"Don't know" responses included in percentage base.

Table 6-17
"What Changes, or Improvements, Would You Like to See Made in the Church You Go to Most Often—That Is, in the Way It's Run, the Services, and So Forth?" Responses of All Protestants, Baptists, and Methodists, by Region; and of Catholics

	Specific Change Mentioned	No Change Needed	Don't Know	(N)
All Protestants				
South	29%	52	19	(681)[a]
Other	31%	49	20	(1376)[a]
Baptists				
South	31%	48	21	(301)[a]
Other	37%	31	32	(144)[a]
Methodists				
South	30%	55	15	(177)[a]
Other	35%	42	23	(318)[a]
Catholics	20%	70	10	(768)[a]

Source: AIPO 660, 1962.
[a]Weighted N. Raw is approximately one-half of this.

needed" may be the Southern equivalent of "don't know." Significantly, *none* of the 681 Southerners said he would like to see his church less "out-of-date," a response volunteered by 18 of the 1376 non-Southerners; further evidence that Southerners do not attribute religion's declining influence to irrelevance.

Effects of Standardization

It might be argued that many of the characteristics of Southern religion are those of the religion of rural, uneducated people generally, so it is necessary to see to what extent the differences shown are due to these factors. Again, standardization can be used to answer this question.

Table 6-18 shows the effects of standardization on regional differences in orthodoxy and in opinions of its necessity. In no case is the reduction striking; there is no reduction in regional difference for two of the four items. The largest reduction—about a third—is in the difference between South and non-South regarding the necessity of literal belief in scripture, although the residuum is still

Table 6-18
Effects of Standardization on Regional Differences in Religious Beliefs

Item	Percentage of Southern Protestants Indicating Belief	Percentage Difference (South)−(Non-South) Unstandardized	Standardized
"Do you believe that Jesus Christ was the Son of God or just a man?" (AIPO 580, 1957)	99%	+ 9	+ 9
"Do you believe that there is or is not life after death?" (AIPO 580, 1957)	89%	+13	+14
"Do you believe that there is or is not a devil?" (AIPO 580, 1957)	86%	+34	+30
"Do you think that a person can be a Christian even if he doesn't believe that every word of the New Testament is true?" (AIPO 580, 1957)	42%	+24	+17

substantial. The large regional differences in what the data reveal to be the relatively peripheral beliefs, then, are only partly due to regional demographic differences, and differences in the more fundamental articles of faith not at all so.

The data on attitudes toward Protestant merger and toward non-Protestants show a similar persistence of regional differences when standardized, although here reduction of the difference is the typical pattern (table 6-19). For all items except the first, standardization reduces the regional differences 20% to 50%, indicating that some part of Southern anti-Semitism and anti-Catholicism *can* be explained by rurality and lack of education. There is, nevertheless, a substantial component of the regional difference in attitudes toward non-Protestants which is not due to these variables. And these factors do not contribute at all to the

Table 6-19
Effects of Standardization on Attitudes Toward Ecumenism and Toward Non-Protestants

Item	Percentage of Southern Protestants Opposed	Percentage Difference (South)−(Non-South)	
		Unstandardized	Standardized
"What is your feeling about [a plan to merge all Protestant churches in the U.S.]?" (AIPO 454, 1950)	62%	+22	+27
"If your party nominated a generally well-qualified man for President and he happened to be a [Catholic], would you vote for him?"[a]	34%	+18	+14
"Would you have a serious objection to a daughter or son of yours marrying a Catholic?" (AIPO 608, 1958)	54%	+14	+ 9
"If your party nominated a generally well-qualified man for President and he happened to be a [Jew], would you vote for him?"[a]	40%	+21	+16
"Would you have a serious objection to a daughter or son of yours marrying a Jew?" (AIPO 608, 1958)	64%	+17	+13
"Do you think [atheists] should be permitted to vote, or not?" (AIPO 714, 1965)	42%	+20	+10

[a]Pooled data from AIPO 604, 649, 714.

regional difference in receptiveness to Protestant merger, which actually increases with standardization. On these items, some strata show substantially greater regional differences than do others, and those strata which differ least from their non-Southern counterparts are, for the most part, urban and/or educated, while those which differ most are not (tables 6-20 and 6-21).

While standardization brings about some reduction—about the same order of magnitude as above—in the relative tendency of Southerners to see church attendance as a necessary part of the Christian life, it makes no difference in Southerners' actual church-going (table 6-22). Here, internal comparisons give some surprising results. The group which differs most from the equivalent group outside the South is that of urban, educated, business and professional people; while one of the groups which differs least is the uneducated farm population

Table 6-20
Proportion Who Would Not Vote for a Well-Qualified Catholic for President, for Selected Standardization Groups, South and Non-South (Protestants Only)

Group[a]	South %	South N	Non-South %	Non-South N	Difference (South)-(Non-South)
Rural, uneducated labor	52	(318)	16	(291)	+35
Urban, uneducated unskilled labor	46	(74)	13	(182)	+33
Urban and town, uneducated business and professional	54	(28)	22	(81)	+31
Town, educated white collar	36	(22)	8	(86)	+28
Town, educated labor	36	(11)	10	(122)	+27
Rural, uneducated business, professional and white collar	42%	(74)	15%	(48)	+27
Urban, educated labor	12	(82)	12	(240)	0
Urban, educated white collar	14	(65)	14	(170)	0
Urban, educated business and professional	13	(94)	15	(296)	− 2
Urban and town, uneducated white collar	9	(11)	18	(89)	− 9

Source: Pooled data from AIPO 604, 649, 714.
[a]All other standardization groups show regional differences of between 6 and 22 percent. Median difference = +13.5; inter-quartile range of differences = 25.

Table 6-21

Proportion Who Would Not Vote for a Well-Qualified Jew for President, for
Selected Standardization Groups, South and Non-South (Christians Only)

Group[a]	South %	South N	Non-South %	Non-South N	Difference (South)-(Non-South)
Town, educated white collar	60	(25)	15	(98)	+45
Town, uneducated skilled labor	54	(13)	12	(89)	+41
Urban and town, uneducated business and professional	48	(27)	12	(154)	+36
Rural, uneducated business, professional and white collar	50	(74)	15	(60)	+35
Urban, uneducated skilled labor	44	(52)	15	(261)	+29
Urban, uneducated unskilled labor	51	(90)	22	(380)	+29
Urban, educated labor	17	(92)	11	(460)	+ 6
Urban and town, uneducated white collar	17	(18)	13	(127)	+ 4
Educated farmers and farm labor	30	(30)	28	(132)	+ 2
Urban, educated white collar	6	(77)	11	(295)	− 5
Town, educated labor	7	(15)	12	(175)	− 5
Town, uneducated unskilled labor	16	(32)	33	(158)	−17

Source: Pooled data from AIPO 604, 649, 714.
[a]All other standardization groups show regional differences of between 10 and 26 percent.
Median difference = +15; inter-quartile range of differences = 25.

(table 6-23). The former group, in the South, is more likely to attend church than the educated, urban white-collar workers—a reversal of the non-Southern association. Responses for the other strata reveal no clear pattern, but it is evident that regional differences in this respect are not at all due to regional demographic differences.

Surprisingly, standardization makes very little difference in the "manners and morals" items. Education, occupation, and rurality account for less than 20% of the regional difference in attitudes toward prohibition and in personal abstinence, and none of the difference in the item concerning feminine modesty (table 6-24).

Examination of the pooled data from three surveys on abstinence (in table

Table 6-22

Effects of Standardization on Regional Differences in Religious Participation

Item	Percentage of Southern Protestants Indicating Participation	Percentage Difference (South)–(Non-South)	
		Unstandardized	Standardized
"Do you think a person can be a (good) Christian if he doesn't go to church?"[a]	32%	+14	+10
Attend church once a week or more (NORC 294, 1950)	42%	+18	+18
Went to church previous week[b]	47%	+11	+11
Listen "regularly" to services on radio or TV (AIPO 580, 1957)	45%	+13	+10

[a]Pooled data from AIPO 580 and 681. The wording on the latter was "good Christian."
[b]Pooled data from AIPO 543, 580, 608, 616, 651, 660, 670, 681.

6-25) reveals, however, that the same group which was disproportionately holding the line on church attendance is the weak link where abstinence is concerned—there is relatively little difference between Southern urban, educated businessmen and professionals and their non-Southern equivalents (although an absolute difference remains). This group is joined in their "un-Southern-ness" in this respect by their educated white-collar employees, and by the educated farmers (of whom it may be said that it is not that they drink so much, but that non-Southern farmers drink so little). The most abstemious strata in the South, when compared stratum by stratum with the non-South, are an odd lot of rural non-farm, and high-status small-town folk—which may reflect more than anything else the existence of local prohibition in parts of the small-town and rural South.

Finally, standardization makes virtually no difference for two items which were discussed above in connection with the church's social role. Table 6-26 presents the data on perceptions of religion's relevance to modern problems and its decreasing influence.

In summary, then, as was the case with localism and with violence, controls for education, occupation, and rurality reduce some of the regional religious differences, but most of each of the differences (and all of some of them) is not due to these factors. Since race and religion have been "controlled" by excluding all but white Protestants, the differences between Southern and non-Southern religion must stem from some other, less obvious, source.

Table 6-23
Proportion Attending Church the Previous Week, for Selected Standardization
Groups, South and Non-South (Protestants Only)

Group[a]	South %	South N	Non-South %	Non-South N	Difference (South)-(Non-South)
Urban, educated business and professional	65	(225)	38	(890)	+27
Town, educated white collar	71	(112)	45	(129)	+26
Rural, uneducated business, professional, and white collar	60	(168)	34	(132)	+26
Urban, uneducated unskilled labor	41	(160)	20	(419)	+21
Rural, educated business, professional and white collar	50	(213)	46	(398)	+ 4
Town, educated skilled and unskilled labor	40	(131)	36	(410)	+ 4
Urban and town, uneducated business and professional	34	(92)	31	(290)	+ 3
Urban, educated white collar	48	(80)	46	(465)	+ 2
Uneducated farmers and farm labor	43	(507)	46	(601)	− 3
Urban and town, uneducated white collar	36	(120)	41	(212)	− 5

Source: Pooled data from AIPO 543, 580, 608, 616, 651, 660, 670, 681.
[a]All other standardization groups show regional differences of between 7 and 17 percent.
Median difference = +9.5; inter-quartile range of differences = 13.

Trend and Outlook: The Non-Withering Away of the Southern Religion

However one attacks the problem, the evidence seems to indicate no substantial decrease in Southern religious peculiarity in the recent past and no prospects for such a decrease in the near future.[48] The available trend data bear this out. Tables 6-1 and 6-2 above show no appreciable change in the religious composition of the South or non-South. The questions on life after death in table 6-3 show, if anything, an increase in Southern orthodoxy (and no corresponding increase for non-Southerners) between 1947 and 1957. Table 6-9 shows no compelling evidence that an apparent decline in Southern church-going has not been

Table 6-24

Effects of Standardization on Regional Differences in Puritanism

Item	Percentage of Southern Protestants Giving Puritan Response	Percentage Difference (South)–(Non-South)	
		Unstandardized	Standardized
Favor national prohibition[a]	48%	+26	+23
Totally abstain from alcohol[b]	67%	+32	+26
Disapprove of women wearing shorts in public (AIPO 651, 1961)	84%	+16	+16

[a]Pooled data from AIPO 580 and 723.
[b]Pooled data from AIPO 543, 580, 723.

Table 6-25

Proportion of Total Abstainers, for Selected Standardization Groups, South and Non-South (Protestants Only)

Group[a]	South		Non-South		Difference (South)-(Non-South)
	%	N	%	N	
Rural, uneducated business, professional and white collar	73	(41)	10	(29)	+63
Urban and town, uneducated business and professional	78	(36)	26	(89)	+52
Rural, educated labor	78	(63)	28	(124)	+50
Town, educated white collar	71	(42)	26	(50)	+45
Urban, educated white collar	41	(39)	28	(152)	+13
Educated farmers and farm labor	63	(54)	53	(136)	+10
Urban, educated business and professional	29	(94)	20	(276)	+ 9

Source: Pooled data from AIPO 543, 580, 723.

[a]All other standardization groups show regional differences of between 19 and 38 percent. Median difference = 26.5, inter-quartile range of differences = 18.

Table 6-26
Effects of Standardization on Regional Differences in Perceptions of Religion in the Modern World

	Percentage of Southern Protestants Agreeing	Percentage Difference (South)−(Non-South)	
		Unstandardized	Standardized
Religion's influences on U.S. life decreasing (AIPO 580, 1957)	21%	+9	+ 8
Religion can answer modern problems (AIPO 580, 1957)	90%	+9	+10

matched by an equivalent decline elsewhere, and table 6-7 may indicate an increase in the difference between Southern Protestants and others in the importance they attach to church attendance (although this is obscured by problems of different question-wordings).

On the questions of sectarianism and hostility to non-Protestants, the trend data are difficult to interpret. Southern receptivity to Protestant merger seems to have decreased between 1950 and 1961, but non-Southern enthusiasm for such schemes seems to have decreased even more, thus substantially narrowing the regional gap (table 6-4). Needless to say, this is not the image of decreasing regional differentiation most mass-society theorists have in mind: the mountain *has* come to Mohammed. The crude measures of anti-Catholic and anti-Jewish prejudice which are available here do show Southern Protestants as moving toward the national norm—they were as liberal in the mid-1960s as the rest of the nation in the mid-1950s, but the norm itself has shifted (table 6-6). Whether or not the regional difference has decreased depends on how the difference is measured: the decreasing percentage difference may be an antifact of the "ceiling effect"—Southerners are *able* to change more, being further from unanimity.

The one unequivocal case of decreasing regional difference revealed by the trend data available here is that with respect to support for national prohibition of the sale of alcoholic beverages. Even this convergence is rendered ambiguous by the lack of a corresponding regional convergence in drinking behavior—where, if anything, the regional difference is increasing (table 6-12). It could very well be that Southerners are becoming, not less puritan, but less attached to lost causes or more consistent in their devotion to States' Rights doctrine. Table 6-12 shows them to have become relatively less willing to vote for a divorced politician, which is not consistent with a hypothesis of increasing moral latitude.

Nothing in these data gives much reason to expect imminent North-South convergence in religious and quasi-religious beliefs and behaviors.

7
The Enduring South

White Southerners continue to display surprisingly strong feelings of attachment to "their people"; in the South, and in the non-South as well, sectional stereotypes are widespread; some degree of sectional feeling is still to be found. This situation *could* prevail in the absence of any real regional distinctions: as legacy from a past in which such distinctions did exist, or, lacking that, as an epiphenomenon of past or present sectional conflict essentially economic in character.[1]

It seems, though, that regional cultural differences have existed and still exist, and that they correspond at least roughly to Americans' perceptions of them. These differences are substantial, and larger than most differences which are thought to be important in the United States. Analyzing a set of survey items (including some of those examined here) chosen to make up "as variegated a set of questions as possible [dealing with] relatively enduring issue[s] judged to be fairly basic and important," Leonard Broom and Norval Glenn report that

in general, Negro-white differences are smaller than the differences between Southern and non-Southern whites. . . . In other words, . . . the population of the United States is apparently somewhat more [culturally] divided along regional . . . than along racial lines."[2]

Using a smaller sample of items (those for which trend data were available), Glenn found South-North cultural differences to be, on the average, larger than those between males and females, urban and rural residents, Protestants and Catholics, manual and non-manual workers, as well as whites and non-whites.[a,3]

In the last three chapters, some of these differences have been examined more closely. Southerners, we have seen, are more likely than non-Southerners to be conventionally religious, to accept the private use of force (or the potential for it), and to be anchored in their homeplace. Although the differences are usually in the same direction as the joint effects of the demographic correlates of Southern-ness, they are too large to be ascribed to these correlates. In the American context and in these respects, in other words, the effect of being Southern is to appear more rural, less educated, and less middle class than one is (or, by Southern standards, the effect of not being Southern is to appear more urban, more educated, and more white-collar than one is).

---

aThe only comparison showing a larger average difference than the regional one was between those with at least some college education and those who had not gone beyond the eighth grade. As Glenn observes, the use of extremes for the educational comparison probably inflates that difference.

Charles O. Lerche has remarked that the "most important single characteristic of the cities of the contemporary South . . . is that—except for climate—there is nothing distinctively Southern about them."[4] The evidence here suggests, to the contrary, that the *people* of these cities remain "distinctively Southern." The differences examined are not consistently concentrated in particular demographic categories. In many respects, Southern middle class urbanites appear to be as different from Northern middle class urbanites as Southern farmers are from Northern farmers. In some respects they are less different, in others more.

There is little indication from our trend data that these differences have decreased appreciably in the recent past. Even for items which have shown considerable fluctuation over time, the *differences* between Southerners and non-Southerners have remained largely constant. Working with a larger pool of items, Norval Glenn has concluded, in fact, that regional differences "probably have increased" recently.[5]

It may be increasingly true, given the undeniable (and overdue) economic development of the South, that "what is left of the old regional differences is . . . a state of mind," but an implicit "merely" is hardly in order.[6] If regional identity, sectional feeling, and cultural difference persist among white Southerners, one must ask why a regionally-based subculture should have maintained its vitality in the face of the supposedly disintegrative and—at the same time—nationalizing tendencies of twentieth-century American mass society.

Sources of Continued Distinctiveness

The characteristics under examination can, with some difficulty, be subsumed by the psychological concept of "authoritarianism," and that label has appealed to at least one serious student of Southern culture.[7] It strains credulity, however, to suggest that Southerners experience "sado-masochistic resolution of the Oedipus complex," resulting in "authoritarian personalities," in sufficiently large numbers to produce the statistical differences we have seen (although one could argue that the regional differences in child-rearing practices leave the possibility open).[8] Others have suggested, as I do here, that "authoritarianism" is as often a cultural style as an attribute of personality, and it is at the cultural and institutional level that we shall look for the explanation of continuing Southern peculiarity.[9]

Some data presented by Glenn and Simmons can be reanalyzed to show that Southern youths are, in many respects, more like their parents' generation than non-Southern youths are like theirs.[10] Coming again from a large and varied set of survey items, the data show a median percentage difference between younger (under 40) and older non-Southern respondents of 9.9, while that for Southern respondents was 4.4.[11] By this measure, the "generation gap" appears to yawn less widely in the South. Before turning to factors which may be operating to perpetuate Southern identity, localism, violence, and religiosity, we ought perhaps to examine the mechanisms by which *any* cultural patterns are maintained and transmitted, since these mechanisms seem to be more efficient in the South than elsewhere.

The attempt in chapter 2 to show that white Southerners can be viewed as an ethnic group was not simply an academic exercise in classification. Other ethnic groups continue to surprise observers by their resistance to assimilation, and the continued survival of white Southerners as a culturally distinct group may be for similar reasons.[12] Both black Americans and immigrant ethnic groups have found in their churches, for instance, a unifying focus and respite from a hostile (or at least strange) majority culture. Most Southern churches are admirably equipped structurally and ideologically (as the Catholic church is not) to serve the same functions for their parishioners, and—as we saw in the last chapter—they seem to do so. Southerners are more likely than other Americans to look to their churches for guidance, and (since the church speaks with a regional accent) they are no more likely than other Americans to find the advice they get distasteful.

Somebody once called Charlestonians "America's Japanese," referring to their habits of eating rice and worshipping their ancestors, and the Southern concern with kin in general is indeed well-known—to the point of stereotype. There does seem to be a basis in fact for this perception: we saw, for instance, in chapter 4, that Southerners are more likely than other Americans to locate normative reference points in their immediate families. This may be self-perpetuating: one of the norms acquired at a Southern mother's knee appears to be that one *should* acquire norms at mother's knee. (In 1953, 74% of Southern respondents to an NORC poll agreed that "the *most important* thing to teach children is *absolute obedience* to their parents," a sentiment shared by somewhat fewer—64%—of the non-Southerners interviewed.)[13] In chapter 5, we saw that there are substantial regional differences in child-rearing practices, and these might also make Southern children more likely to adopt their parents' values, although the effects of different discipline techniques on the transmission of diffuse cultural characteristics are little understood.[14]

In the traditional view of the American "melting pot," the schools were assigned an important role in weaning the children of immigrants from their parents' ways and assimilating them into the majority culture. Although some are beginning to suspect that the schools never did this job very well, it does seem undeniable that, simply by placing these children in classrooms with already assimilated teachers and often with assimilated classmates, the schools have in the past contributed to cultural uniformity. By naive analogy, some observers seem to have expected Southerners similarly to be assimilated by mass education. The fallacy, of course, is that by and large neither teachers nor students in Southern schools are "already assimilated"—they are themselves Southerners and share Southern values. (About two-thirds of Southern high school teachers hold degrees from colleges in the state in which they are teaching.)[15] Although the effects of desegregation remain to be seen, the result in the past has been something within the public school system closely akin to a parochial school, with similarly conservative effects.

Even if Southern teachers might wish to subvert community values, their ability to do so would seem to be limited. The principle of academic freedom has historically had little acceptance in the South, even at the college level (at one time recently, exactly half of the institutions on the American Association of University Professors blacklist were Southern), and the alternative idea of teachers' unionism has not made much headway either.[16]

A different role-definition may combine with prudence to prevent Southern teachers' departing from their areas of professional competence. A recent study has shown Southern teachers less likely than teachers elsewhere to say that a teacher "should feel free" to engage in political discussion or activity in the classroom (or in the community): to what extent this reluctance extends to other non-academic expressions is unknown.[17]

Finally, even if Southern teachers did not share community values, felt it was legitimate to impart others, and could try to do so without fear for their jobs, their attempts might be less efficacious than those of non-Southern teachers, since teachers may be held in lower esteem in the South. Although an NORC study of occupational prestige showed negligible regional differences in ratings of "school teachers" and "college professors," in 1951 only 35% of white Southerners under forty said they would prefer a son to be a $4000 a year college professor rather than a $6000 a year factory foreman, while 49% of white non-Southerners under forty chose the former.[18] All in all, the Southern school system does not appear to be a formidable rival of the Southern family for the job of socializing the South's children.

The situation is similar in the case of the mass media. Although regional differences in media exposure (presently operating to reduce the relative influence of the media in the South) will probably vanish with increasing education and urbanization, there is little reason to suppose that the contribution of such exposure to regional uniformity will be overwhelming. As in the case of the school system, the staff of the media in the South is largely Southern, often with a sensitivity to community sentiment similar to that of the teachers. True, much of the content of the media is not locally originated, but some screening is exercised at the local level, and control over emphasis and placement of material is entirely in local hands. In newspapers, for instance, the nationally syndicated columnists are likely to be chosen with an eye to local feeling. (Most textbooks in Southern schools bear Northern imprints, as well, but choice and interpretation may reflect local values.) In a case study of Northern and Southern newspaper coverage of the Emmett Till lynching, Warren Breed found very little difference in the actual information conveyed, but considerable difference in exactly these respects: style, emphasis, and tacit values.[19]

Once wire service material reaches print, or network material gets on the air, the familiar processes of selective exposure, perception, interpretation, and retention operate to mitigate its impact still further.[20] According to figures of the A. C. Nielson Company, only one program, "The Lucy Show," was among the top ten programs for both the South and the Northeast in 1967.[21] (Southerners prefer "countrified situation comedies and Westerns"; Northeasterners "citified variety shows" and "movies, originally made for a more sophisticated theater audience." Region, dichotomized in this way, seems to make more difference in viewing practices than income or occupation, and the regional difference is about the same as that between those with a grade school education only and those with at least some college education.)

Finally, the media seem to be taken less seriously outside the Northeast—or at least "radio announcer," "newspaper columnist," and "daily newspaper reporter" are less prestigious occupations in the South, Midwest and West.[22] This would seem to lessen their potential effect on the cultural patterns of their audiences.

The point is not that the media are exceptionally subservient to community values in the South (although they may be), it is merely that their homogenizing effects may have been overrated. To the extent that these effects exist, they may act primarily *within* regions rather than *across* them. Thus, Glenn finds that urban-rural differences in the United States, unlike regional differences, have been decreasing.[23]

In summary, then, two institutions, the family and the church, are more powerful in the South than elsewhere in the United States. Two others, the school and the media, seem relatively less influential. The first two are more culturally conservative generally, and may be particularly so in the South. Of the last two, at least the school is more "community-controlled" in the South, with the culturally conservative function such control implies. There is an interesting circularity here, if one accepts these generalizations: the very cultural differences which set the South apart foster differences in institutional arrangements which insure that those cultural differences (and others) will persist.

These arguments alone do not imply, however, that regional convergence will not occur, much less that regional differences will grow larger, but merely that the erosion of the Southern subculture will be retarded. We might expect that (as is the case with white Southern racial attitudes) even if few persons change their minds and most children take on their parents' attitudes and values, what "breakage" does occur will be in the direction of decreasing regional differences.[24] The effects of migration should also work to produce convergence. If the South is becoming *less* like the rest of the country (or, for that matter, if the rest of the country is becoming less like the South), it is certainly not what one would expect from the simplistic application of mass-society notions. If regional convergence is not occurring, if regional differences are actually increasing in some respects, factors other than social inertia must be brought into the explanation.

Southern Culture As Defense

The question of where regional differences came from in the first place is logically distinct from that of why they continue to exist, and a sociologist is tempted to leave the first question with the historians, simply accepting their judgment that the differences we have been looking at were well-established by 1860. As Arthur Stinchcombe has observed, however, the same social forces which bring a social fact into being may act to perpetuate it once it is established.[25] For this reason, it may be worth inquiring after continuities in the historical experience of white Southerners.

David L. Smiley has remarked that "in the history of Southern history, the central theme has been the quest for the central theme"—some single factor which can explain the nature of the South and even, some have hoped, the course of Southern history.[26] Causal importance has been attributed to dozens of factors, ranging from the obvious "givens" of climate and soil, through the type of agriculture and the slave labor force which climate and soil made desirable, the style of life which staple crops and black labor made possible, and the political and military conflict which somehow evolved from all of this.[27] With a few notable exceptions, the theorists of the central theme have been lamentably unclear about the causal connections of these factors with each other and with the facts to be explained.

Running through many of these writings, however, and captured entire by several of them, is an image of the South which, if it has been accurate—or, rather, if Southerners have *felt* it to be accurate—can account for the characteristics we have been examining. The image is one of a people defined in opposition to a powerful, external threat. C. Vann Woodward has spoken of the antebellum South's feeling of isolation and insecurity, "its conviction that it was being encircled and menaced from all sides."[28] The experiences of the subsequent century evidently did little to allay this conviction, for we find Charles Lerche writing of the present-day Southerner's enemy: "outsiders," who commit "the unpardonable sin of bringing the South and its problems to the attention of the nation and the world." "Southerners feel," he claims, "that they are struggling against an open conspiracy and a totally hostile external environment and that they can never receive a fair hearing."[29] Sheldon Hackney has identified a "sense of grievance . . . at the heart of the Southern identity," and has sketched its history:

The South was created by the need to protect a peculiar institution from threats originating outside the region. Consequently, the Southern identity has been linked from the first to a seige mentality. [Southerners see themselves] defending their region against attack from outside forces: abolitionists, the Union Army, carpetbaggers, Wall Street and Pittsburgh, civil rights agitators, the Federal Government, feminism, socialism, trade unionism, Darwinism, communism, atheism, daylight savings time, and other by-products of modernity. . . .

"Being Southern," he concludes, "inevitably involves a feeling of persecution at times and a sense of being a passive, insignificant object of alien or impersonal forces."[30] With the reservation that few Southerners have ever acknowledged that they were passive or insignificant, Hackney's is an admirable statement of the observation that many Southerners seem to feel (as many, it appears, have always felt) that hundreds of thousands of "meddlers" are conspiring to undermine the South's institutions and the "Southern way of life." This contributed to the formation of the Southern identity ("It is not a country at all," Karl Marx said of the Confederacy, "but a battle slogan"[31]), and underlies that identity today. It would be called paranoiac were it not essentially correct: in a region which has had at least its share of the American experience of rapid social change, one constant has been that nearly all of that change has been imposed from outside.[32] It is not merely a truism to observe that there would be no South if there were no North.

And, if the wider world is perceived as sharing a consensus that one's inherited way of living is immoral and inferior (particularly if one has secret doubts of his own), if the wider world is viewed as unreasonable and unpersuadable, what is more understandable than to ignore the "wider world" as best one can, and seek support and validation from family and community?[33] If the world threatens what one cherishes (or even simply what one finds convenient and congenial) and seems deaf to pleas for understanding, cannot that be taken to support the view that force is not just a last resort, but the only one?[34] If institutional structures permit it, who could resist enlisting the moral authority of religion in the service of threatened values (and what churches are more deserving of support than ones which provide such comfort)?

While this is a caricature of the Southern situation, the features it exaggerates are real ones. Localism, violence, and a conservative religion are all plausible responses for a minority group, surrounded by a culture which is viewed as powerful, hostile, and unresponsive; all can be seen as adaptive reactions to the situation in which Southerners have, time and again, found themselves. I am suggesting that these defenses, mobilized in the antebellum sectional crisis, have been sustained by the chronic crisis which has been Southern history since.

This is not to say that such responses are inevitably the effects of external threat on a culture, although some other threatened cultures—French Canadians, for instance, the Irish, American Negroes—have responded similarly. Adaptation to threat must build on preexisting tendencies in the culture, and these were the historical givens for Southerners. Nor is it necessary to assert that all or even most Southerners feel threatened much of the time, merely that enough feel threatened enough of the time to keep these responses a part of the general regional culture (where they will be shared by threatened and secure alike). Sectional conflict serves the two purposes of intensifying group identity and providing the threat which can emphasize the "functionality" of Southern culture.[35]

Other "outside" threats can serve the second purpose just as well, and there is some evidence that Southerners have, of late, generalized the threatening outside to include foreign enemies of the United States.[36]

"Save Just a *Little Bit* of Your Confederate Money, Boys"

For a long time to come, we can expect that the South will be something more than simply the lower right-hand part of the country. Although the region is, in some respects, rejoining the Union at last, the accommodation is a tentative one. Southerners continue to see themselves as others see them, as *different*—and, in some ways, they are different.

Perhaps it was naive to expect social and economic change to obliterate regional differences. The South has been undergoing social and economic change, off and on, for most of its history, and regional differences have shown remarkable resilience. The idea that "modernization" by its nature must produce uniformity seems to rest on an exaggerated view of what the regional differences are. South and North are, after all, much more like one another than either is like Japan, or Russia; the Southern culture seems comfortably within the range of those consistent with urban, industrial society.

As for "mass culture": one of the differences between South and North seems to be that the former is, by institutional arrangement, more resistant to the culture of mass society. One can hardly suppose that these arrangements, and the values which support them, will change overnight under the impact of that same mass culture.

Finally, if their culture serves Southerners, for better or worse, in dealing with a hostile "outside," it will probably continue to serve so long as the outside seems to be hostile. The traditional outside has been the North, and the occasion for sectional animosity has usually been the South's racial institutions (although other issues have served at times): if the South's race relations improve or the North's deteriorate, white Southerners may yet realize their ancient wish to be "let alone."

Yet C. Vann Woodward has doubted out loud that the nation will ever lose its need for a scapegoat, or ever find another as satisfactory as the South, and—apart from that—it seems unlikely that a nation as large and varied as the United States will long be without conflicting sectional interests.[37] If Southerners should find their collective interests or their pride in jeopardy, no one should be surprised if the old back-to-the-wall imagery is resurrected, the tattered battle flags unfurled, the God of Hosts invoked, and the words of an antebellum circus poster are apt yet again:[38]

Southern Men
Southern Horses
Southern Enterprise
AGAINST THE WORLD!!!

Methodological Appendix

Methodological Appendix

1. Secondary Analysis of Sample Surveys

The survey data used here were not collected with this study in mind. They come from various public opinion polls, taken over the last three decades and thoughtfully stored for further analysis in social science data archives. I hope that this study may be of some interest—aside from its substance—as an example of "secondary analysis," illustrating both the unique possibilities and inherent limitations of this approach.

The obvious virtue of secondary analysis, of course, is its economy. For about what a single interview costs today, the secondary analyst can obtain the results of more than a thousand interviews. These data come, moreover, from representative national samples, which makes them admirably suited for the study of social groupings as large and varied as "regions." Community studies, or analyses of speeches, editorials, and other entries in the public record, are hazardous bases for inferences about a regional culture: the representativeness of the data base is always subject to challenge. Since the survey organizations' sampling procedures guarantee that all areas and population strata will be represented, the grounds for doubt on this score are substantially reduced, and the question of representativeness becomes, in fact, a technical and statistical one.

The price one pays for this economy is the loss of a great deal of control over what data are gathered. The secondary analyst's ingenuity is sometimes insufficient to produce a fit between the variables he is concerned with and those the survey organizations have thought to collect. Since the quantity of secondary data available is increasing exponentially with time, however, this may be less of a problem in the future. In any event, the analyst must be prepared to trade something for the extended coverage of time and space which secondary analysis provides.

The analyst must also give up some measure of control (and sometimes even knowledge) of how the data are gathered. It is not simply that a commercial firm's procedures may not be up to an academic researcher's utopian standards: the analyst may be unable to discover what the procedures were in the first place. Survey organizations' gift horses are often close-mouthed—some, in fact, regard their sampling techniques as trade secrets. Since they are paying for the data-collection, however, the secondary analyst should probably be willing to trust that they are looking out for their interests—which happily coincide with his since their continued prosperity rests on being accurate most of the time.

Herbert Hyman, in his monograph *Secondary Analysis of Sample Surveys*, has discussed the many methodological advantages which accrue to the secondary analyst, and anyone interested in pursuing the subject should certainly consult that volume. Several of the advantages which Hyman discusses, which have been particularly exploited here, stem from the fact that many questions have been asked more than once.

For instance, responses to the same question asked at different times give some insight into the problem of response stability, a question which may be related to that of item validity. If the analyst is inferring the existence of cultural traits from opinion items, it is disconcerting if responses show erratic fluctuation over time. To be sure, a radical change in the marginal distribution of responses from one time to another does not necessarily indicate low stability (or little change, high stability), but in the absence of alternative explanations, one is alerted to the possibility. If the item has been asked more than twice, a smooth curve is more reassuring in this respect than abrupt shifting about.

More substantively, time series data are an aid in assessing the meaning of the latest situation. One way of addressing the question of whether a proportion (or a difference in two proportions) is "large" or "small" is to compare it to what it has been in the past.

Often, of course, the time series itself is of interest. If one is concerned with the past change in a statistic, whether for essentially historical purposes or as a basis for projection, secondary analysis is by far the best of the available techniques. (Compare it, for instance, to estimation from documentary sources, or the inclusion of retrospective items in a current survey.) Even if an hypothesis could be studied by a primary trend study, secondary analysis commends itself as a means of extending the trend for more years than are practical otherwise, since the time-span covered by archived data will soon exceed an individual's productive lifetime.

Finally, repeated asking of the same or similar questions allows one, in effect, to replicate findings. The usual advantages of replication accrue. In particular, a slight difference which turns up in several independent samples makes one less ready to ascribe it to sampling error.

These advantages of secondary analysis of repeated items assume that the different surveys are kept separate. In the present analysis, results have been shown separately for different polls, in order to benefit from these considerations. In several instances, however, data from different surveys have then been *pooled* in order to build up the size of some subsamples of interest. For instance, by pooling responses to three separate surveys, we can get enough Southern, white, Protestant, urban, white-collar high school graduates to examine their drinking behavior, and compare it to that of *Northern* white, Protestant, urban, white-collar high school graduates. Where a question has been asked a great many times (as has one on church attendance, for instance), one could go on stratifying much further than I have.[a]

The data analyzed here (except for the Matthews-Prothro data examined in chapter 2) were obtained from the Roper Public Opinion Research Center, prob-

---

[a]Pooling, for the purposes of this study, does *not* require that there be no change in the dependent variable, but it does require that such change occur uniformly in the population or that the effects of differential change offset each other.

ably the best-known and certainly the largest repository of survey data in the world. (For a succinct description of the Roper Center's operations and holdings, see Alfred O. Hero, Jr., *The Southerner and World Affairs*, pp. 643-48.) For the most part, the surveys for analysis were chosen "blind," without prior knowledge of the results: the only exceptions were those containing items which this analysis has in common with Norval Glenn and J. L. Simmons, "Are Regional Cultural Differences Diminishing?" and the search procedure was such that these surveys would have been included in any event.

Documentation for some of the early surveys was somewhat sketchy, and one problem arose in consequence: although black respondents were excluded, respondents whose race was coded "3" (where "1" was white and "2" black) were not. There is no indication of what this code denoted and, although there were relatively few of these respondents (usually less than 5% of the "white" sample in the earlier years and none in the later), there were sometimes more of them than of "Negro" respondents. Their position on various items which discriminate sharply between black and white respondents was usually intermediate. It would be helpful in cases like this if the analyst had access to the original interview schedules (although the storage problems for the archives would be immense). The point is underlined by the fact that several open-ended questions of interest were not coded at all, coded inconsistently over time, or otherwise made less useful than they might have been. As Hyman observes, a secondary analyst with access to the uncoded data could rework them for his own purposes.

Other technical problems arose from the fact that the analysis drew on many surveys. Since nearly all of the data were collected by one organization, the American Institute of Public Opinion, we do not have to contend with variation introduced by different organizations' different precedures, but during the thirty years from which the data come this one organization has changed its methods several times. Norval Glenn has discussed some of these changes and their implications in his article in the *Public Opinion Quarterly*, "Problems of Comparability in Trend Studies with Public Opinion Poll Data." Since there is little reason to suppose that these changes have *systematically* affected the regional differences under examination, I shall mention them only in passing:

1. Some of the early polls did not contain all of the background items necessary for the standardization.

2. Early in the period under consideration, the Institute changed from a sampling scheme which included Southerners at their *voting* weight (about 10% of the white respondents) to one which included them in numbers proportional to their weight in the general population (about 20% of the white respondents). This change makes no difference for present purposes, although Southern figures for the earlier period are, in general, based on smaller numbers of respondents.

3. Toward the end of the period, the Institute changed to a form of sample which is weighted for education and "at-homeness." This procedure counts the

uneducated and the seldom-home more heavily than other respondents, to make up for the fact that such persons are under-represented in samples drawn conventionally. This may have affected the gross regional differences, since the uneducated are a larger proportion of the Southern population, but education is controlled in the standardization. The figures for the later period (those based on "weighted N's") are more *reliable* than the earlier ones.

Since many items came from the same questionnaires, and since the sampling design was often only approximately known, I have not computed tests for statistical significance. The bases on which the percentages were computed are included in the tables to give a rough idea of the stability of the figures shown, and readers who are concerned about statistical significance should consult Glenn's "Problems of Comparability" article. The best argument for the validity of the data, it seems to me, is their internal consistency, and the frequent replication which was possible.

2. Test-Factor Standardization

One view of regional cultural differences holds that most are due to regional differences in demographic and economic variables. Some scholars seem to feel (although they would not put it this baldly) that most Southern cultural peculiarities (they might exempt Southerners' racial views) are a direct result of the Southern population's being relatively uneducated, rural, and unindustrialized. They would argue, in other words, that regional cultural differences are *spurious*.[b] This explanation of regional differences is appealingly simple, and deserves examination: certainly regional comparisions should be shown with education, rurality, and occupation controlled. The method used in the text to perform this control is "test-factor standardization." Morris Rosenberg has described the technique, long familiar to demographers, in "Test Factor Standardization as a Method of Interpretation," but some description of how it works may be in order here.

The nature of standardization is perhaps best conveyed by example. Suppose we have samples from the populations of two countries, Ruritania and Urbana. In Ruritania, 35% of the 200 respondents support the Socialist Party, while 65% of Urbana's 200 respondents support their Socialists. One possible explanation of the difference is that Urbana is much more urban than Ruritania. If we run

[b]This is an extension of the usual meaning of the word "spurious" as applied to an association between two variables (here, region and some cultural indicator). Occupation, rurality, and education form what Hyman calls, in *Survey Design and Analysis*, pp. 260-62, a "configuration" with the subcultural aspects of region, neither causally antecedent to nor intervening between region and its supposed effects. One might say, however, that these factors are *theoretically* "antecedent" to region: we feel more comfortable attributing effects to them than to region since there is a more highly developed rationale for doing so. In any event, controlling for them allows the analyst to attribute any residual effects of region to other aspects of the configuration than these.

the three-variable table, party preference by rurality for each country (table A), we can see that *all* of the difference in support for the Socialists is due to differences in the rural-urban distribution of the two countries.

Standardization begins with the data displayed in table A, and addresses the question: What would the level of support in each country be *if they had the same level of urbanization*? It requires that this "same level" be specified—that some common base be chosen. For example, we could ask what the two countries would look like if each were entirely urban. Obviously, if that were the case, 80% of each country's population would support the Socialists. We could ask what they would look like if each country were 50% urban: In each country, 80% of the urban half and 20% of the rural half, or 50% altogether, would support the Socialists.

If we prefer, we can treat the two populations asymmetrically. We may suspect that Urbana represents what Ruritania will look like in a few decades. If so, it makes sense to ask what level of support the Socialists could expect if Ruritania were as urban as Urbana is now—in other words, to standardize Ruritania to the distribution displayed by Urbana. If 75% of Ruritania's population were urban and 80% of Ruritania's urban population continued to support the Socialists; if only 25% of the population were rural and 20% of this population continued to support the Socialists; then the level of Socialist support in this hypothetical population would be 80% of the urban 75% plus 20% of the rural 25%, or 65% altogether—the same as the present level of support in Urbana.

In this example, it makes no difference what base we use to standardize the two populations. The initial difference of 30% is reduced to zero, no matter what base is used. This is not true in general, however. The amount of reduction of the initial difference may depend on what base is chosen. In table B, for instance, there is no association between the control variable and the dependent variable in Ruritania. No matter what base we use to standardize Ruritania's distribution, the marginal distribution of party preference will not change. The amount of change, if any, in the distribution for Urbana, and hence in the percentage difference, will depend on the base chosen.

The choice of a base implies a model, and standardization will be misleading

Table A

Party Preference by Residence, in Two Nations (Hypothetical Data)

| | Percentage Supporting Socialists | |
Residence	Urbana	Ruritania
Rural	20%	20%
(N)	(50)	(150)
Urban	80%	80%
(N)	(150)	(50)
TOTAL	65%	35%
(N)	(200)	(200)

Table B

Party Preference by Residence, in Two Nations (Hypothetical Data)

	Percentage Supporting Socialists	
Residence	Urbana	Ruritania
Rural	20%	35%
(N)	(50)	(150)
Urban	80%	35%
(N)	(150)	(50)
TOTAL	65%	35%
(N)	(200)	(200)

to the extent that the model is inappropriate. In the present analysis, I have standardized the South so that it looks, demographically, like the non-South. This reflects the evidence that this is the general direction of demographic change in the United States, and is a more reasonable assumption, I think, than that which would be implicit in standardizing the non-South to the South, or both the South and the non-South to the aggregate distribution for the United States—or that for Bulgaria.

In the examples above, standardization adds nothing to the tables presented. They are easily read as they stand. The real usefulness of standardization becomes apparent, however, when the control variable is not dichotomous. If the analyst is controlling for a variable which has a great many possible values, each value will generate a "partial table," showing the association between independent and dependent variable under that condition. Standardization provides, in effect, a convenient and sensible method for "averaging" the partial associations, giving an indication of the amount of the initial two-variable association which is explained or interpreted by the control variable. In fact, the percentage difference after standardization here can be shown to be a weighted average of the percentage differences in the partial tables, weighted by the proportion of the "base" population in each of the control categories. If one wishes to control for several variables simultaneously, the simplest procedure is to use them to construct a typology, and control for this typology, treating it as a nominal variable. Standardization is admirably suited for this application.

In the present analysis, simultaneous controls were desired for three variables: respondents' education, place of residence (rural, town, or urban), and occupation. The variables, defined in table C, were used to construct the typology shown in table D. (Data from surveys which did not allow the control variables to be broken in this fashion—or did not contain them at all—were not standardized.) The typology was constructed by an essentially hit-or-miss procedure, guided by two general criteria.

Since the South was to be standardized to look like the North, I tried to avoid generating types which would be vastly more frequent in the North than in the South. It would obviously be undesirable to have a category which was, say,

Table C

Breaks on the Constituent Variables of the Control Variable

Variable	Category	AIPO Code Categories
Residence:	rural	farm resident open country, non-farm
	town	places under 2,500 2,500 to 4,999 . . . 25,000 to 49,999
	urban	50,000 to 99,999 and suburbs . . . 1,000,000 and over and suburbs
Education:	"uneducated"	None or grades 1-4 . . . High school, incomplete (grades 9-11)
	"educated"	High school, grad. (grade 12) Tech., trade, or bus. school College, university, incomplete College, university, grad.
Occupation: (of household head)	business and professional	professional business, executive
	white collar	clerical sales worker
	skilled labor[a]	skilled workers
	unskilled labor[a]	unskilled workers, operatives service workers laborers, except farm and mine
	farm	farmers farm laborers
	undesignated	non-labor-force undesignated

[a]The category "labor," when used, combines these two.

20% of the non-Southern population and 2% of the Southern. Standardization would, in this case, greatly inflate the sampling error of the figure. (It can be shown that, in any event, the standard error of the standardized proportion will be greater than or equal to that of the unstandardized proportion.)[c]

In addition, I attempted (on impressionistic and—when possible—empirical

[c]One easily demonstrated fact about standardization is that if two types are in the same ratio *to each other* (not necessarily to the total population) in the two populations, they may be combined without affecting the results of the standardization. This result is of less use in constructing types than might be supposed, however, since the proportions of each type in the two populations vary from survey to survey, due both to actual demographic change in the populations and to sampling error.

Table D

Categories of the Control Variable

Type	Residence	Occupation	Education
I	urban	business and professional	educated
II	town	business and professional	educated
III	urban and town	business and professional	uneducated
IV	urban	white collar	educated
V	town	white collar	educated
VI	urban and town	white collar	uneducated
VII	urban	labor	educated
VIII	town	labor	educated
IX	urban	skilled labor	uneducated
X	urban	unskilled labor	uneducated
XI	town	skilled labor	uneducated
XII	town	unskilled labor	uneducated
XIII	–	farm	educated
XIV	–	farm	uneducated
XV	rural	business and professional; white collar	educated
XVI	rural	business and professional; white collar	uneducated
XVII	rural	labor; undesignated	educated
XVIII	rural	labor; undesignated	uneducated
XIX	urban	undesignated	educated
XX	urban	undesignated	uneducated
XXI	town	undesignated	educated
XXII	town	undesignated	uneducated

grounds) to maximize cultural homogeneity *within* types and maximize variability *across* types.

The resulting typology has several shortcomings. The second criterion above had to yield to the realities of sample size and the actual distribution of the United States population. In particular, the measures of the constituent variables are crude (education is dichotomized at high school graduation, for instance). Some comfort may perhaps be taken from the fact that the three variables are interrelated: variance in education which is ignored by the dichotomization will still be controlled to the extent that it is associated with occupation and rurality.

Another possible objection has to do with the non-comparability of the control variables in the two regions—a high school education in the South, it may be, is not equivalent to a high school education elsewhere. If this is taken to mean that the two are not comparable in their effects on the dependent variables, that is precisely what is being examined, so the objection is the same as our hypothesis. On the other hand, if what is meant is that the amount of *education*—measured, say, by standardized tests—is not the same, that is another matter. Similarly, if one objects that Southern urbanites are more likely to be recent migrants from rural areas, he may be correct. Whether these objections are germane depends on what it is about education or urban life that is supposed to be affecting values, a question I cannot address here.

A somewhat more sophisticated objection, and an entirely valid one, is that this procedure, while controlling for the direct effects of education, rurality, and occupation on the dependent variables, does not control for their *contextual* effects. Southerners are less educated, more rural, less in white-collar occupations: these factors are controlled. They are also living with people who are less educated, etc., than are the people non-Southerners live with: these indirect, or contextual, effects of the South's demography are *not* controlled. If the contextual effects are in the same direction as the direct effects, standardization may *understate* the change which could be expected if the South came to resemble the non-South. This limitation should be kept in mind when evaluating the conclusions of this inquiry.

All of these limitations would apply to any multivariate approach to the same data, however. They are not unique to standardization or to the particular control variable being employed. They can only be frankly acknowledged, and the case for the defense put on an empirical basis.

It may be instructive to work through an example of standardization using the control variable employed in this analysis. Not only will it be of some use in explicating the technique, but the example will be one in which the initial North-South difference is shown to be largely due to demographic differences, as measured by the control variable.

In 1966, the Gallup Poll asked: "If you could live anywhere in the United States that you wanted to, would you prefer a city, suburban area, small town, or farm?" (AIPO 723). Of the Southern respondents, 32% said they would prefer a farm; of the Northerners, 14% did so. Table E gives the data necessary to standardize the South to the North's demographic distribution. This is accomplished, mechanically, by simply multiplying the percentage of Southerners in each category who would prefer farm life by the number of non-Southerners in that category, adding up the products, and dividing by the total number of Northerners. If the South had the same distribution over the types as the North has now, and if Southerners of each type retained their present likelihood of responding "farm," 20% of this hypothetical Southern population would prefer to live on a farm—closer to the North's present 14% than to the South's present 32%. (Some confidence in the control variable may be established by noting that, even with a crude trichotomization of rurality, it explains the North-South

Table E

Components of Standardization for Example (See Text)

Type	Proportion of Southerners Desiring to Live on Farm	(N)[a]	Number of Non-Southerners in Category
I	.053	(95)	357
II	.316	(38)	59
III	.000	(13)	87
IV	.000	(31)	164
V	.105	(19)	40
VI	.316	(19)	83
VII	.050	(40)	320
VIII	.167	(18)	90
IX	.182	(33)	81
X	.069	(29)	136
XI	.000	(3)	48
XII	.294	(17)	103
XIII	.417	(12)	83
XIV	.884	(43)	47
XV	.383	(47)	77
XVI	.706	(17)	26
XVII	.652	(46)	102
XVIII	.609	(133)	158
XIX	.000	(17)	134
XX	.259	(27)	163
XXI	.000	(13)	21
XXII	.000	(33)	61
			2440

[a]This figure is not necessary for the computation, but is included to give an idea of the reliability of the corresponding proportion. N's in this column and the next are weighted; raw are approximately one-half as large.

difference better than an uncollapsed measure of rurality—10 categories—alone. Standardizing for the latter gives a figure for the South of 27%.)

For this application, standardization is clearly preferable to tabular analysis: it summarizes, in effect, the twenty-two two-variable tables—no small service. Its other desirable features can be illuminated by comparing it to a rather more sophisticated alternative, analysis of covariance. First, and most important, standardization has a simple and appealing operational interpretation. The logic of the "thought experiment" which it embodies is more readily accessible to readers without statistical training than is the notion of "covariance explained." Even so, it has some desirable statistical properties. One can exploit the possible asymmetry of the technique and make use, for instance, of the knowledge that the South is coming to resemble the North, and not vice versa. A related advantage of standardization, as it is employed here, is that it ignores interaction. The first question to be addressed is simply: What happens if the South is made to look like the North? Interaction, if present, may help explain the results of the standardization, but its consideration is a *subsequent* procedure.

When possible, I have not altogether ignored interaction between region and the control variable. When the bases for the 22 partial tables could be built up to meaningful numbers by pooling data from several surveys, I have done so. The question addressed in the text of "what strata in the South differ most (and least) from the equivalent strata in the North" *is* the question of interaction. If none were present, North-South differences should be about the same for all strata. As a rough measure of interaction, I have appended the inter-quartile range of North-South differences to the tables showing differences by strata: this statistic should approach zero if there is no interaction in the table.

3. Regional Definitions

The regional divisions used by the American Institute of Public Opinion are:

South
  North Carolina
  South Carolina
  Virginia
  Georgia
  Alabama
  Arkansas
  Florida
  Kentucky
  Louisiana
  Mississippi
  Oklahoma
  Tennessee
  Texas

New England
  Maine
  New Hampshire
  Vermont
  Massachusetts
  Rhode Island
  Connecticut

East Central
  Ohio
  Michigan
  Indiana
  Illinois

West Central
  Wisconsin
  Minnesota
  Iowa
  Missouri
  North Dakota
  South Dakota
  Nebraska
  Kansas

Mountain States
  Montana
  Arizona
  Colorado
  Idaho
  Wyoming
  Utah
  Nevada
  New Mexico

Middle Atlantic
  New York
  New Jersey
  Pennsylvania
  'Maryland
  Delaware
  West Virginia

Pacific Coast
  California
  Oregon
  Washington

The National Opinion Research Center uses the Census Bureau's regional divisions. Their "South" includes, besides the states listed above, Maryland, West Virginia, Delaware, and the District of Columbia; the "Eastern States" are AIPO's "New England," plus New York, New Jersey, and Pennsylvania. NORC's "Central States" are the same as AIPO's; and "the West" the same as AIPO's "Mountain States" and "Pacific Coast."

Bibliography

Bibliography

The notes to each chapter (following this bibliography) will give some guidance to readers who wish to locate works which amplify points made in the text or which present different views. Since I have attempted in the text and in the notes themselves to indicate the pertinence of the works cited, those cited often or other than incidentally are merely listed here, for reference.

The general social science literature, while by no means exhausting the relevant material, will serve as a reasonably good introduction for the non-professional reader to the conceptual and methodological underpinnings of studies like this one.

Needless to say, the works on the South cited here are only the tip of *that* iceberg—actually, only one side of the tip. The sketchy treatment given the work of economists, political scientists, demographers, and human ecologists reflects a rather different subject matter, not a neglect of the South by those disciplines or any shortcomings in their studies of the region. Some fine historical writing was, for present purposes, adequately summarized in historiographical reviews and is not otherwise cited. Much excellent material, notably social anthropologists' vignettes of several Southern communities, lacked a sufficiently explicit comparative dimension or was too specific to a particular subculture within the South to be included. Finally, although the sensitive and often brilliant journalism devoted to the South has shaped the thinking of anyone who has read it, methodological scruples prevented my drawing on it (other than for colorful turns of phrase) as heavily as I might have.

In short, many of the most important contributions to our understanding of the South are not cited here, and the reader who is unfamiliar with this literature and interested in pursuing it should turn to a good introductory bibliography such as that in Louis D. Rubin, Jr., ed., *A Bibliographical Guide to the Study of Southern Literature*, pp. 3-10; or that in Alfred O. Hero, Jr., *The Southerner and World Affairs*, pp. 619-43. The first half of the Rubin volume is an invaluable collection of specialized bibliographies on various aspects of Southern culture; the remainder deals with specific Southern writers. Two other specialized bibliographic works listed here are Link and Patrick, eds., *Writing Southern History* — the Southern historian's *vade mecum*; and Odum and Jocher, eds., *In Search of the Regional Balance of America*, pp. 60-86 of which contain a bibliography of "regionalist" social science through the early 1940s.

Bailey, Kenneth K. *Southern White Protestantism in the Twentieth Century*. New York: Harper and Row, 1964.
Bertrand, Alvin L. "Regional Sociology as a Special Discipline." *Social Forces* 31 (December 1952): 132-36.
Billington, Monroe L., ed. *The South: A Central Theme?* New York: Holt, Rinehart and Winston, 1969.

Brearley, H.C. "The Pattern of Violence." In *Culture in the South*, edited by W.T. Couch. Chapel Hill: University of North Carolina Press, 1934.

Breed, Warren. "Comparative Newspaper Handling of the Emmett Till Case." *Journalism Quarterly* 35 (Summer 1958): 291-98.

Brown, George H. "The New South." Address to International Conference on Population Priorities and Options for Commerce and Industry, Chapel Hill, N.C., 23 October 1970.

Brown, Robert Raymond. "Southern Religion, Mid-Century." In *The Lasting South*, edited by Louis D. Rubin, Jr., and James Kilpatrick. Chicago: Henry Regnery Company, 1957.

Campbell, Angus; Converse, Philip E.; Miller, Warren E.; and Stokes, Donald E. *The American Voter: An Abridgement*. New York: John Wiley & Sons, Inc., 1964.

Campbell, Ernest, and Pettigrew, Thomas. *Christians in Racial Crisis: A Study of Little Rock's Ministry*. Washington: Public Affairs Press, 1959.

Cash, W.J. *The Mind of the South*. New York: Alfred A. Knopf, 1941.

Coser, Lewis A. *The Functions of Social Conflict*. London: Free Press of Glencoe, 1964.

Couch, W.T., ed. *Culture in the South*. Chapel Hill: University of North Carolina Press, 1934.

Fichter, Joseph H., and Maddox, George L. "Religion in the South, Old and New." In *The South in Continuity and Change*, edited by John C. McKinney and Edgar T. Thompson. Durham: Duke University Press, 1965.

Fishbein, Martin, ed. *Readings in Attitude Theory and Measurement*. New York: John Wiley & Sons, Inc., 1967.

Franklin, John Hope. *The Militant South, 1800-1861*. Cambridge: Harvard University Press, 1956.

Gastil, Raymond D. "Homicide and a Regional Culture of Violence." *American Sociological Review* 36 (June 1971): 412-27.

Gillin, John. "National and Regional Cultural Values in the United States." *Social Forces* 34 (December 1955): 107-13.

Glenn, Norval D. "Massification versus Differentiation: Some Trend Data from National Surveys." *Social Forces* 46 (December 1967): 172-80.

―――. "Problems of Comparability in Trend Studies with Opinion Poll Data." *Public Opinion Quarterly* 34 (Spring 1970): 82-91.

―――, and Simmons, J.L. "Are Regional Cultural Differences Diminishing?" *Public Opinion Quarterly* 31 (Summer 1967): 176-93.

Gordon, Milton M. *Assimilation in American Life: The Role of Race, Religion, and National Origins*. New York: Oxford University Press, 1964.

Gouldner, Alvin W. "Cosmopolitans and Locals: Toward an Analysis of Latent Social Roles—I." *Administrative Science Quarterly* 2 (1957-58): 281-306.

Grantham, Dewey W., ed. *The South and the Sectional Image: The Sectional Theme Since Reconstruction*. New York: Harper and Row, 1967.

Hackney, Sheldon. "Southern Violence." *American Historical Review* 74 (February 1969): 906-25.

Harwell, Richard B. "The Stream of Self-Consciousness." In *The Idea of the South: Pursuit of a Central Theme*, edited by Frank E. Vandiver. Chicago: University of Chicago Press, 1964.

Heberle, Rudolf. "Regionalism: Some Critical Observations." *Social Forces* 21 (March 1943): 280-86.

Hero, Alfred O., Jr. *The Southerner and World Affairs*. Baton Rouge: Louisiana State University Press, 1965.

Hertzler, J.O. "Some Notes on the Social Psychology of Regionalism." *Social Forces* 18 (March 1940): 331-37.

_____. "Some Sociological Aspects of American Regionalism." *Social Forces* 18 (October 1939): 17-29.

Hill, Samuel S., Jr. "An Agenda for Research in Religion." In *Perspectives on the South: Agenda for Research*, edited by Edgar T. Thompson. Durham: Duke University Press, 1967.

_____. *Southern Churches in Crisis*. New York: Holt, Rinehart and Winston, 1966.

Hyman, Herbert H. *Secondary Analysis of Sample Surveys: Principles, Procedures, and Potentialities*. New York: John Wiley & Sons, Inc., forthcoming.

_____. *Survey Design and Analysis*. Glencoe, Ill.: The Free Press, 1955.

_____, and Sheatsley, Paul B. "Attitudes toward Desegregation." *Scientific American* 211 (July 1964): 16-23.

_____. "Some Reasons Why Information Campaigns Fail." *Public Opinion Quarterly* 11 (Fall 1947): 413-23.

_____, and Singer, Eleanor, eds. *Readings in Reference Group Theory and Research*. New York: The Free Press, 1968.

Jennings, M. Kent, and Zeigler, L. Harmon. "Political Expressivism among High School Teachers: The Intersection of Community and Occupational Values." In *Learning About Politics: A Reader in Political Socialization*, edited by Roberta S. Sigel. New York: Random House, [1970].

_____. "The Salience of State Politics Among Attentive Publics." Paper read at Annual Meeting of the American Political Science Association, 1968.

Jensen, Merrill, ed. *Regionalism in America*. Madison: University of Wisconsin Press, 1951.

Katz, Daniel, and Braley, Kenneth. "Racial Stereotypes of One Hundred College Students." *Journal of Abnormal and Social Psychology* 28 (October-December 1933): 280-90.

Key, V.O., Jr. *Southern Politics in State and Nation*. New York: Alfred A. Knopf, 1949.

Killian, Lewis. *White Southerners*. New York: Random House, 1970.

Lerche, Charles O., Jr. *The Uncertain South: Its Changing Patterns of Politics in Foreign Policy*. Chicago: Quadrangle Books, 1964.

Link, Arthur S., and Patrick, Rembert W., eds. *Writing Southern History: Essays in Historiography in Honor of Fletcher M. Green*. Baton Rouge: Louisiana State University Press, 1965.

McKinney, John C., and Bourque, Linda Brookover. "The Changing South: National Incorporation of a Region." *American Sociological Review* 36 (June 1971): 399-412.

_____, and Thompson, Edgar T., eds. *The South in Continuity and Change*. Durham: Duke University Press, 1965.

Mack, Raymond, ed. *The Changing South*. Chicago: Aldine Publishing Company, Trans-action Books, 1970.

Manschreck, Clyde L. "Religion in the South: Problem and Promise." In *The South in Perspective*, edited by Francis B. Simkins. Farmville, Va.: Longwood College, 1959.

Matthews, Donald R., and Prothro, James W. *Negroes and the New Southern Politics*. New York: Harcourt, Brace & World, Inc., 1966.

Mayo, Selz C. "Social Change, Social Movements, and the Disappearing Sectional South." *Social Forces* 43 (October 1964): 1-10.

Merton, Robert K. *Social Theory and Social Structure*. Rev. ed. New York: Free Press of Glencoe, 1957.

_____, and Rossi, Alice Kitt. "Contributions to the Theory of Reference Group Behavior." In *Readings in Reference Group Theory and Research*, edited by Herbert H. Hyman and Eleanor Singer. New York: The Free Press, 1968.

Metzger, L. Paul. "American Sociology and Black Assimilation: Conflicting Perspectives." *American Journal of Sociology* 76 (January 1971): 627-47.

Myrdal, Gunnar. *An American Dilemma*. Twentieth Anniversary ed. New York: Harper and Row, 1962.

Nicholls, William H. *Southern Tradition and Regional Progress*. Chapel Hill: University of North Carolina Press, 1960.

Odum, Howard W. "Notes on the Study of Folk and Regional Society." *Social Forces* 10 (December 1931): 1-12.

_____. *Southern Regions of the United States*. Chapel Hill: University of North Carolina Press, 1936.

_____. *The Way of the South*. New York: The Macmillan Company, 1947.

_____, and Jocher, Katherine, eds. *In Search of the Regional Balance of America*. Chapel Hill: University of North Carolina Press, 1945.

_____, and Moore, Harry Estill. *American Regionalism: A Cultural-Historical Approach to National Integration*. New York: Henry Holt and Company, 1938.

Olmsted, Frederick Law. "Slavery in its Effects on Character and the Social Relations of the Master Class." In *The Cotton Kingdom: A Traveller's Observations on Cotton and Slavery in the American Slave States*. New York: Alfred A. Knopf, 1962.

Phillips, Ulrich B. "The Central Theme of Southern History." *American Historical Review* 34 (October 1928): 30-43.

Poteat, Edwin McNeill, Jr. "Religion in the South." In *Culture in the South*, edited by W.T. Couch. Chapel Hill: University of North Carolina Press, 1934.

Potter, David. *The South and the Sectional Conflict*. Baton Rouge: Louisiana State University Press, 1968.

Rappeport, Michael A. "Trends in American Political Behavior." Paper read at Conference of American Association for Public Opinion Research, 1970.

Reed, John Shelton. "Continuing Distinctiveness in Southern Culture." *University of North Carolina News Letter* 55 (December 1970).

_____. " 'The Cardinal Test of a Southerner': Regional Identity and its Correlates." In *The Search for Group Identity: Concern for Community and Region in the South*, edited by Harold F. Kaufman, et al. Forthcoming.

Reiss, Albert J., Jr. (with Duncan, Otis Dudley; Hatt, Paul K.; and North, Cecil C.). *Occupations and Social Status*. Glencoe, Ill.: The Free Press, 1961.

Reissman, Leonard. "Social Development and the American South." *Journal of Social Issues* 22 (January 1966): 101-16.

Rosenberg, Morris. "Test Factor Standardization as a Method of Interpretation." *Social Forces* 41 (October 1962): 53-61.

Royce, Josiah. *Race Questions, Provincialism, and Other American Problems*. New York: The Macmillan Company, 1908.

Rubin, Louis D., Jr., ed. *A Bibliographical Guide to the Study of Southern Literature*. Baton Rouge: Louisiana State University Press, 1969.

_____, and Kilpatrick, James Jackson, eds. *The Lasting South: Fourteen Southerners Look at Their Home*. Chicago: Henry Regnery Company, 1957.

Rymph, Raymond C., and Hadden, Jeffrey K. "The Persistence of Regionalism in Racial Attitudes of Methodist Clergy." *Social Forces* 49 (September 1970): 41-50.

Simkins, Francis Butler. "The Rising Tide of Faith." In *The Lasting South*, edited by Louis D. Rubin, Jr., and James Jackson Kilpatrick. Chicago: Henry Regnery Company, 1957.

_____, ed. *The South in Perspective*. Farmville, Va.: Longwood College, 1959.

Smiley, David L. "The Quest for the Central Theme in Southern History." Paper read at Conference of the Southern Historical Association, 1962.

Stark, Rodney, and Glock, Charles Y. *American Piety: The Nature of Religious Commitment*. Berkeley: University of California Press, 1968.

Stinchcombe, Arthur L. *Constructing Social Theories*. New York: Harcourt, Brace & World, 1968.

Tindall, George B. "The Benighted South: Origins of a Modern Image." *Virginia Quarterly Review* 40 (Spring 1964): 281-94.

_____. *The Emergence of the New South, 1913-1945*. Vol. 10 of *A History of the South*, edited by Wendell Holmes Stephenson and E. Merton Coulter. Baton Rouge: Louisiana State University Press, 1967.

_____. "Mythology: A New Frontier in Southern History." In *The Idea of the South: Pursuit of a Central Theme*, edited by Frank E. Vandiver. Chicago: University of Chicago Press, 1964.

de Tocqueville, Alexis. *Democracy in America* 1. Translated by Henry Reeve. New Rochelle, N.Y.: Arlington House, n.d.

Vance, Rupert B. "The Concept of the Region." *Social Forces* 8 (December 1929): 208-18.

_____, and Demerath, Nicholas J., eds. *The Urban South*. Chapel Hill: University of North Carolina Press, 1954.

Vandiver, Frank E. "The Southerner as Extremist." *The Idea of the South: Pursuit of a Central Theme*. Chicago: University of Chicago Press, 1964.

Weaver, Richard M. *The Southern Tradition at Bay: A History of Postbellum Thought*. New Rochelle: Arlington House, 1968.

Westbrook, John T. "Twilight of Southern Regionalism." *Southwest Review* 42 (Summer 1957): 231-34.

Woodward, C. Vann. "From the First Reconstruction to the Second." In *The South Today: 100 Years after Appomattox*, edited by Willie Morris. New York: Harper Colophon Books, 1966.

Zelinsky, Wilbur. "An Approach to the Religious Geography of the United States: Patterns of Church Membership in 1952." *Annals of the Association of American Geographers* 51 (June 1961): 139-93.

Notes

Notes

Preface

1. T.H. Marshall, *Class, Citizenship, and Social Development* (Garden City, N.Y.: Doubleday & Co., 1964), p. 38.
2. David Potter, *The South and the Sectional Conflict* (Baton Rouge: Louisiana State University Press, 1968), pp. 181-182.

Chapter 1
"Yes, but Not in the South"

1. New York: Holt, 1950, p. 27.
2. Rupert B. Vance, "Beyond the Fleshpots: The Coming Culture Crisis in the South," *Virginia Quarterly Review* 41 (Spring 1965): 222.
3. Leonard Reissman, "Social Development and the American South," *Journal of Social Issues* 22 (January 1966): 115.
4. New York: W.W. Norton & Company, 1957; Joseph B. Cummings, Jr., "Been Down Home So Long It Looks Like Up to Me," *Esquire*, August 1971, pp. 84 ff.
5. "Social Development and The American South," p. 102. For instance: Thomas D. Clark, Jr., *The Emerging South*, 2nd ed. (London: Oxford University Press, 1968); R.B. Highshaw, ed., *The Deep South in Transformation* (University: University of Alabama Press, 1964); Allan P. Sindler, ed., *Change in the Contemporary South* (Durham: Duke University Press, 1963); Raymond W. Mack, ed., *The Changing South* (Chicago: Transaction Books, Aldine Publishing Company, 1970); John M. Maclachlan and Joe S. Floyd, Jr., *This Changing South* (Gainesville: University of Florida Press, 1954).
6. George H. Brown, "The New South," address to International Conference on Population Priorities and Options for Commerce and Industry, Chapel Hill, N.C., 23 October 1970, p. 1.
7. See, for instance, John C. McKinney and Linda Brookover Bourque, "The Changing South: National Incorporation of a Region," *American Sociological Review* 36 (June 1971): 399-412; Sanford Labovitz and Ross Purdy, "Territorial Differentiation and Societal Change in the United States and Canada," *American Journal of Economics and Sociology* 29 (April 1970): 127-47; Sanford Labovitz, "Regional Analysis of the United States" (M.A. thesis, University of Texas, Austin, 1962); Selz C. Mayo, "Social Change, Social Movements, and the Disappearing Sectional South," *Social Forces* 43 (October 1964): 1-10.
8. McKinney and Bourque, "The Changing South," p. 408.
9. The metaphor is David Potter's; *The South and the Sectional Conflict*, p. 4.

10. *Race Questions, Provincialism, and Other American Problems* (New York: The Macmillan Company, 1908), pp. 74-75. More recent treatments include Francis E. Merrill, *Society and Culture: An Introduction to Sociology*, 4th ed. (Englewood Cliffs, N.J.: Prentice-Hall, Inc., 1969), pp. 393-411; and Milton M. Gordon, *Assimilation in American Life: The Role of Race, Religion, and National Origins* (New York: Oxford University Press, 1964), p. 50, an explicit discussion of regional differentiation.

11. John T. Westbrook, "Twilight of Southern Regionalism," *Southwest Review* 42 (Summer 1957): 232.

12. Ulrich B. Phillips, "The Central Theme of Southern History," *American Historical Review* 34 (October 1928): 31.

13. J.S. Reed, "Continuing Distinctiveness in Southern Culture," *University of North Carolina News Letter* 55 (December 1970). Cf. Herbert H. Hyman and Paul B. Sheatsley, "Attitudes toward Desegregation," *Scientific American* 211 (July 1964): 16-23; American Institute of Public Opinion, *Gallup Opinion Index*, Report No. 59 (May 1970), pp. 4-5.

14. Michael A. Rappeport, "Trends in American Political Behavior" (paper read to Conference of American Association for Public Opinion Research, 1970), p. 5.

15. Ibid., p. 6. Cf. E.M. Schreiber, " 'Where the Ducks Are': Southern Strategy versus Fourth Party," *Public Opinion Quarterly* 35 (Summer 1971): 157-67.

16. John C. McKinney and Edgar T. Thompson, eds., *The South in Continuity and Change* (Durham: Duke University Press, 1965); Louis D. Rubin, Jr., and James Jackson Kilpatrick, eds., *The Lasting South: Fourteen Southerners Look at Their Home* (Chicago: Henry Regnery Company, 1957); Francis Butler Simkins, *The Everlasting South* (Baton Rouge: Louisiana State University Press, 1963). Other doubters include William H. Nicholls, *Southern Tradition and Regional Progress* (Chapel Hill: University of North Carolina Press, 1960); Fletcher Melvin Green, "Resurgent Southern Sectionalism, 1933-1955," in *Democracy in the Old South and Other Essays by Fletcher Melvin Green*, ed. J. Isaac Copeland (Nashville: Vanderbilt University Press, 1969), pp. 288-306; Robin M. Williams, Jr., "Unity and Diversity in Modern America," *Social Forces* 36 (October 1957): 1-8, especially p. 2; C. Vann Woodward, "From the First Reconstruction to the Second," in Willie Morris, ed., *The South Today: 100 Years after Appomattox* (New York: Harper Colophon Books, 1966), p. 1-14; Edwin M. Yoder, "W.J. Cash after a Quarter Century," ibid., pp. 89-99.

17. Paul Gaston, *The New South Creed: A Study in Southern Mythmaking* (New York: Alfred A. Knopf, 1970). Henry Grady's original "New South" address was given in 1886: it is reprinted in *The New South and Other Addresses* (New York: Charles E. Merrill Co., 1904), pp. 23-42.

18. Norval D. Glenn and J.L. Simmons, "Are Regional Cultural Differences Diminishing?" *Public Opinion Quarterly* 31 (Summer 1967): 176-93.

19. See the distinction in Gordon, *Assimilation in American Life*, pp. 79-80, between *extrinsic* and *intrinsic* cultural patterns.

20. Unless otherwise noted, survey data used here were supplied through the courtesy of the Roper Public Opinion Research Center, Williamstown, Massachusetts. Most were collected by the American Institute of Public Opinion (AIPO), better known as "the Gallup Poll." Two of the surveys were conducted by the National Opinion Research Center (NORC). References to these surveys will be by name of agency (AIPO or NORC), the agency's number, and date (e.g., AIPO 580, 1957).

21. "Some Sociological Aspects of American Regionalism," *Social Forces* 18 (October 1939): 27.

22. For example, community studies such as John Dollard, *Caste and Class in a Southern Town* (New Haven: Yale University Press, 1937); Allison Davis, Burleigh B. Gardner, and Mary R. Gardner, *Deep South: A Social Anthropological Study of Caste and Class* (Chicago: University of Chicago Press, 1941); Liston Pope, *Millhands and Preachers* (New Haven: Yale University Press, 1942)—a study of religious life in a Southern mill town; Morton Rubin, *Plantation County* (Chapel Hill: University of North Carolina Press, 1951); and two studies of the white population of the town of "Kent": John Kenneth Morland's *Millways of Kent* (Chapel Hill: University of North Carolina Press, 1958) and Ralph C. Patrick, Jr., "A Cultural Approach to Social Stratification," (Ph.D. diss., Harvard University, 1953). An ambitious attempt to put these together with community studies from other parts of the United States and extract the uniquely regional aspects of culture can be found in John Gillin, "National and Regional Cultural Values in the United States," *Social Forces* 34 (December 1955): 107-113.

23. The cultural atypicality of the South may be obvious. If not, it is an implication of the data in Glenn and Simmons, "Are Regional Cultural Differences Diminishing?" The relative homogeneity of the non-Southern regions provides a rationale for grouping them as the "non-South."

24. "Research Design," in Robert Ward, ed., *Studying Politics Abroad: Field Research in the Developing Areas* (Boston: Little, Brown, 1964), p. 162.

25. Herbert H. Hyman, *Survey Design and Analysis* (Glencoe, Ill.: The Free Press, 1955), pp. 126-31, is primarily concerned with the use of related variables to evaluate a distribution, but indicates the usefulness of readings on the same variable for a related population (p. 131).

26. Bulgaria has been used, as a matter of fact. See Irwin T. Sanders, "Bulgarians and Southern Rural Whites in Contrast," *Social Forces* 19 (October 1940): 88-94.

27. Cf. Robert K. Merton, *Social Theory and Social Structure*, rev. ed. (New York: Free Press of Glencoe, 1957), pp. 421-36.

Chapter 2
Southerners: Who, What, and Where

1. For a discussion of "region" in this sense, see Alvin Bertrand, "Regional Sociology as a Special Discipline," *Social Forces* 31 (December 1952): 132-36;

Hertzler, "Some Sociological Aspects of American Regionalism"; and especially J.O. Hertzler, "Some Notes on the Social Psychology of Regionalism," *Social Forces* 18 (March 1940): 331-37. Considering its demonstrable importance as an explanatory variable, there has been little systematic examination of region by social psychologists.

2. M. Kent Jennings and L. Harmon Zeigler, "The Salience of State Politics among Attentive Publics" (paper read at annual meeting of the American Political Science Association, 1968). Since "region" is often considered to be a property of *states* in political science research, perhaps the serious evaluation of it as an individual characteristic comes more naturally to political scientists.

3. See, for instance, Rupert B. Vance, "The Concept of the Region," *Social Forces* 8 (December 1929): 208-18. Rudolf Heberle sketches the intellectual history of regionalism in "Regionalism: Some Critical Observations," *Social Forces* 21 (March 1943): 280-82. A more extended treatment can be found in Howard W. Odum and Harry Estill Moore, *American Regionalism: A Cultural-Historical Approach to National Integration* (New York: Henry Holt and Company, 1938), pp. 277-419.

4. For a discussion of this distinction, see the introduction to Herbert H. Hyman and Eleanor Singer, eds., *Readings in Reference Group Theory and Research* (New York: The Free Press, 1968), pp. 9-11; and Robert K. Merton and Alice Kitt Rossi, "Contributions to the Theory of Reference Group Behavior," ibid., pp. 33 ff.

5. New York: Random House, 1971.

6. *Assimilation in American Life*, pp. 27-29.

7. Ibid., p. 40.

8. Ibid., p. 38.

9. For a description of the study (field work conducted by the Survey Research Center of the University of Michigan) see Matthews and Prothro, *Negroes and the New Southern Politics* (New York: Harcourt, Brace & World, Inc., 1966), pp. 489-95. Their data were obtained for analysis from the Inter-University Consortium for Political Research, through the Louis Harris Political Data Center at the University of North Carolina, Chapel Hill. The initial use of the items is reported in Angus Campbell et al., *The American Voter: An Abridgment* (New York: John Wiley & Sons, Inc., 1964), pp. 168-71. Group identification among white Southerners is examined in more detail in J.S. Reed, " 'The Cardinal Test of a Southerner': Regional Identity and its Correlates," forthcoming in Harold F. Kaufman et al., eds. *The Search for Group Identity: Concern for Community and Region in the South.*

10. The ethnic homogeneity of the Southern white population, while relatively great, should not be exaggerated, however. See John Maclachlan, "Distinctive Cultures in the Southeast: Their Possibilities for Regional Research," *Social Forces* 18 (December 1939): 210-15; John Kenneth Morland, ed., *The Not So Solid South: Anthropological Studies in a Regional Subculture*, Southern Anthropological Society Proceedings, No. 4 (Athens: University of Georgia Press, 1971).

11. See, for instance, the review article by Martin Fishbein, "Attitude and the Prediction of Behavior," in his edited volume, *Readings in Attitude Theory and Measurement* (New York: John Wiley & Sons, Inc., 1967), pp. 477-92.

12. *Race Questions, Provincialism, and Other American Problems*, p. 61.

13. Cf. Herbert H. Hyman, "Dimensions of Social Psychological Change in the Negro Population," mimeographed chapter prepared for forthcoming volume edited by Angus Campbell and Philip E. Converse, December 1968, pp. 39 ff.

14. Quoted in Heberle, "Regionalism: Some Critical Observations," p. 283.

15. "Notes on the Study of Regional and Folk Society," *Social Forces* 10 (December 1931): 3-4. Compare, e.g., his "Folk and Regional Conflict as a Field of Sociological Study," *Publication of the Sociological Society of America* 25 (May 1931): 9-11; or Odum and Moore, *American Regionalism*, pp. 417-18.

16. The concerns of the Chapel Hill group can be inferred from a sampling of the titles of their published work: Odum's "Regional Development and Governmental Policy," *The Annals*, November 1939, pp. 133-41; his *Regional Approach to National Social Planning* (New York: Foreign Policy Association, 1935); his "Case for Regional National Social Planning," *Social Forces* 13 (October 1934): 6-23; Rupert Vance, "Human Resources and Public Policy: An Essay toward Regional-National Planning," ibid. 22 (October 1943): 20-25; Edith Webb Williams, "Research and Regional Development: An Inquiry into the Range and Role of Research in the South," ibid. 23 (March 1945): 350-56; James W. Fesler, "Criteria for Administrative Regions," ibid. 22 (October 1943): 26-32; and George Simpson and John E. Ivey, Jr., "Regionalism and Social Planning: A Footnote to the Organic Role of Regionalism in National Planning," ibid. 20 (December 1941): 185-95. The list could be extended indefinitely: see Odum and Katherine Jocher, eds., *In Search of the Regional Balance of America* (Chapel Hill: University of North Carolina Press, 1945), pp. 61-86.

17. For treatments of the subject of regional definition, see, for instance, Odum and Moore, *American Regionalism*, pp. 2-34 et passim; Svend Riemer, "Theoretical Aspects of Regionalism," *Social Forces* 21 (March 1943): 275-80; Edward L. Ullman, "Human Geography and Area Research," *Annals of the Association of American Geographers* 43 (March 1953): 57-61; and Werner J. Cahnman, "Outline of a Theory of Area Studies," ibid. 38 (December 1948): 234-35 et passim.

18. Two one-index studies of particular interest are Rexford Newcomb, "Regionalism in American Architecture," and Hans Kurath, "Linguistic Regionalism," in Merrill Jensen, ed., *Regionalism in America* (Madison: University of Wisconsin Press, 1951), pp. 273-95 and 297-310. Each finds the South's northern boundary to take in southern Ohio, Indiana, and Illinois, due to historical settlement patterns (pp. 284, 303). Cf. Wilbur Zelinsky, "Where the South Begins: The Northern Limit of the Cis-Appalachian South in Terms of Settlement Landscape," *Social Forces* 30 (December 1951): 172-78.

19. *Southern Regions of the United States* (Chapel Hill: University of North Carolina Press, 1936). See the partial listing on p. 4.

120

20. Phenomena with less extensive distributions can be used to define *subregions*. Southern subregions, ignored here, are treated in Rupert B. Vance, *Human Geography of the South* (Chapel Hill: University of North Carolina Press, 1932).

21. For other forms of integration which might be used, but have not been, see Werner S. Landecker, "Types of Integration and Their Measurement," *American Journal of Sociology* 56 (January 1951): 332-40.

22. *Southern Regions*, pp. 6-9.

23. AIPO 582.

24. For further evidence on New Englanders' distaste for Southern accents, see G. Richard Tucker and Wallace E. Lambert, "White and Negro Listeners' Reactions to Various American-English Dialects," *Social Forces* 47 (June 1969): 463-68.

25. U.S. Bureau of the Census, *Historical Statistics of the United States, Colonial Times to 1957; Continuation to 1962 and Revisions* (Washington: U.S. Government Printing Office, 1965), Series C 15-24.

26. Hyman and Sheatsley, "Attitudes toward Desegregation," pp. 22-23.

Chapter 3
"The South of the Mind": Regional
Attitudes and Stereotypes

1. These data are also from AIPO 582.

2. The literature on the subject is too extensive for review here. See, for example, James S. Coleman, *Community Conflict* (New York: The Free Press, 1957); Philip E. Converse, "The Shifting Role of Class in Political Attitudes and Behavior," in Eleanor E. Maccoby et al., eds., *Readings in Social Psychology*, 3rd ed. (New York: Holt, Rinehart and Winston, Inc., 1958), pp. 388-99.

3. These data are not shown, since the associations are slight. Reed, " 'The Cardinal Test of a Southerner,' " shows that the correlates of anti-Northern sentiment and of Southern identity are not exactly the same.

4. This would be suggested by several different social-psychological theories of "cognitive consistency." For a review of these theories, see William J. McGuire, "The Current Status of Cognitive Consistency Theories," in Fishbein, ed., *Attitude Theory and Measurement*, pp. 401-21.

5. *An American Dilemma*, Twentieth Anniversary Edition (New York: Harper and Row, 1962), p. 1037.

6. From codebook for AIPO 582, supplied by Roper Center.

7. Many historians have written ably on this subject. See the sources in James B. Colvert, "The South in Northern Eyes," in Louis D. Rubin, Jr., ed., *A Bibliographical Guide to the Study of Southern Literature* (Baton Rouge: Louisiana State University Press, 1969), pp. 76-78; George Tindall, "Mythology: A

New Frontier in Southern History," in Frank E. Vandiver, ed., *The Idea of the South: Pursuit of a Central Theme* (Chicago: University of Chicago Press, 1964), pp. 1-15.

8. Ibid.; D. Potter, *The South and the Sectional Conflict*, pp. 4-9. Cf. Howard W. Odum, *An American Epoch* (New York: Henry Holt Company, 1930), pp. 330-31.

9. "Moral alchemy" is Robert K. Merton's phrase. See his discussion of this process in *Social Theory and Social Structure*, pp. 426-430.

10. Tindall, "Mythology," pp. 3-5.

11. Quoted in T. Harry Williams, *Romance and Realism in Southern Politics* (Athens: University of Georgia Press, 1960), p. 10.

12. David Bertelson, *The Lazy South* (New York: Oxford University Press, 1967).

13. "Slavery in its Effects on Character and the Social Relations of the Master Class," reprinted in Olmsted, *The Cotton Kingdom: A Traveller's Observations on Cotton and Slavery in the American Slave States*, ed. Arthur M. Schlesinger (New York: Alfred A. Knopf, 1962), p. 614.

14. Ibid.

15. *Democracy in America*, trans. Henry Reeve, 1 (New Rochelle, N.Y.: Arlington House, n.d.), p. 356.

16. Some of these pro-slavery writings have been collected in Eric L. McKitrick, ed., *Slavery Defended: The Views of the Old South* (Englewood Cliffs, N.J.: Prentice-Hall, Inc., Spectrum Books, 1963). An interpretation of the thought of one of the most fascinating of these writers, George Fitzhugh, is given by Eugene Genovese, in *The World the Slaveholders Made* (New York: Random House, Vintage Books, 1971), pp. 118-244.

17. "Slavery in its Effects," pp. 616, 618.

18. Ibid., pp. 616, 615.

19. Ibid., p. 615.

20. Edmund Clarence Stedman to his mother, reprinted in Henry Steele Commager, ed., *The Blue and the Grey: The Story of the Civil War as Told by Participants* (Indianapolis: The Bobbs-Merrill Company, Inc., 1950), p. 54.

21. For a sensitive discussion of Southern politics at mid-century, see Odum, *The Way of the South: Toward the Regional Balance of America* (New York: The Macmillan Company, 1947), pp. 197-207.

22. "The Benighted South: Origins of a Modern Image," *Virginia Quarterly Review* 40 (Spring 1964): 281-94.

23. Cf. the similar observation by Ralph Bunche, quoted in Myrdal, *American Dilemma*, p. 962, fn. a.

24. Edith Oliver, review of "Day of Absence," *The New Yorker*, 28 March 1970, p. 84.

25. James B. Colvert, "Views of Southern Character in Some Northern Novels," *Mississippi Quarterly* 18 (Spring 1965): 59-68.

122

26. Thomas F. Pettigrew, "Complexity and Change in American Racial Patterns: A Social-Psychological View," in Talcott Parsons and Kenneth B. Clark, eds., *The Negro American* (Boston: Beacon Press, 1967), p. 335.

27. On media treatment of Southerners, see Woodward, "From the First Reconstruction to the Second," p. 13. On the general public's lapses from cordiality, see Killian, *White Southerners*, pp. 32-33, 91-119 (esp. 108-109), et passim; Raymond Mack, "Is the White Southerner Ready for Equality?" in Mack, *The Changing South*, pp. 9-20.

Chapter 4
"Down Home": Southern Localism

1. *The Way of the South*, pp. 61-62.

2. See D. Potter, *The South and the Sectional Conflict*, p. 15. John McKinney and Charles P. Loomis discuss the general concept in "The Application of Gemeinschaft and Gesellschaft As Related to Other Typologies," the introduction to Ferdinand Toennies, *Community and Society (Gemeinschaft und Gesellschaft)*, trans. C.P. Loomis (East Lansing: Michigan State University Press, 1957), pp. 12-29. E.K. Francis, in "The Nature of the Ethnic Group," *American Journal of Sociology* 52 (March 1947): 393-400, discusses the relation of the concepts "folk" and "ethnic group." "Folk culture" is used here solely in the sense of "preindustrial culture."

3. Talcott Parsons, *The Social System* (New York: The Free Press of Glencoe, 1951), pp. 61-63 et passim.

4. "Communicating with the Educationally Deprived," *Mountain Life and Work* 42, no. 1 (1966): 10. See Florence R. Kluckhohn and Fred L. Strodtbeck, *Variations in Value Orientations* (Evanston, Ill.: Row, Peterson, 1961), pp. 1-48.

5. Richard B. Harwell, "The Stream of Self-Consciousness," in Vandiver, *The Idea of the South*, pp. 17-25; Charles S. Sydnor, *The Development of Southern Sectionalism, 1819-1848,* vol. 5 of Wendell Holmes Stephenson and E. Merton Coulter, eds., *A History of the South* (Baton Rouge: Louisiana State University Press, 1948), esp. pp. 294-339; Avery O. Craven, *The Growth of Southern Nationalism, 1848-1861*, vol. 6, ibid. (1953).

6. The Agrarians are best represented by themselves—see their manifesto, *I'll Take My Stand: The South and the Agrarian Tradition*, by Twelve Southerners (New York: Harper and Brothers, 1930). Virginia Rock has compiled a bibliography on "Agrarian Themes and Ideas in Southern Writing," in Rubin, *Bibliographical Guide to the Study of Southern Literature*, pp. 119-127, which traces their precursors and successors and lists the critical works. On the Regionalists, see Dewey W. Grantham, Jr., "The Regional Imagination: Social Scientists and the American South," *Journal of Southern History* 34 (February 1968): 3-32; George B. Tindall, *The Emergence of the New South, 1913-1945*, vol. 10 of Stephenson and Coulter, eds., *History of the South* (1967), pp. 582 ff.

7. Clifford Dowdey, "The Case for the Confederacy," in Rubin and Kilpatrick, eds., *The Lasting South*, pp. 29-30.

8. See D. Potter, *The South and the Sectional Conflict*, pp. 34-83, for a sensitive discussion of Southerners' conflicting loyalties.

9. "Politics," *Esquire*, October 1968, p. 246.

10. William Albig, *Public Opinion* (New York: McGraw-Hill Book Company, 1939), pp. 165, 169.

11. Jennings and Zeigler, "The Salience of State Politics among Attentive Publics," pp. 26, 29.

12. See V.O. Key, Jr., *Southern Politics in State and Nation* (New York: Alfred A. Knopf, 1949), for an overview of the region's old-time political factions. For a more recent survey, see Kevin P. Phillips, *The Emerging Republican Majority* (New Rochelle, N.Y.: Arlington House, 1969), pp. 187-289.

13. Phillips, *Emerging Republican Majority*, passim.

14. Key, *Southern Politics*, passim—e.g., pp. 37-39. Comparative data for non-Southern states are lacking.

15. See Rubin, ed., *Bibliographical Guide to the Study of Southern Literature*; idem, *Writers of the Modern South: The Faraway Country* (Seattle: University of Washington Press, 1963), pp. 3-20.

16. Merton, *Social Theory and Social Structure*, pp. 392 ff.

17. D. Potter, *The South and the Sectional Conflict*, pp. 34-83; or, for that matter, Edmund Burke, *Reflections on the Revolution in France* (1790), passim.

18. On normative reference processes, see Hyman and Singer, *Readings in Reference Group Theory and Research*, especially the article by Harold H. Kelley, "Two Functions of Reference Groups," pp. 77-83.

19. For the census data, see U.S. Bureau of the Census, *Historical Statistics of the United States*, Series C 15-24.

20. E.g., Nicholls, *Southern Tradition and Regional Progress*, especially pp. 34-42.

21. For a summary and history of the "colonial" analogy, see Tindall, *Emergence of the New South*, pp. 594-605.

22. Allan M. Carter, *An Assessment of Quality in Graduate Education* (Washington, D.C.: American Council on Education, 1966), pp. 107 ff.

Chapter 5
"To Live—and Die—in Dixie": Southern Violence

1. Sheldon Hackney, "Southern Violence," *American Historical Review* 74 (1969): 906. See p. 906, fn. 1, for references to representative comments.

2. Rupert B. Vance, "The Geography of Distinction: The Nation and Its Regions 1790-1927," *Social Forces* 18 (December 1939): 175-76 (figures 3 and 4).

3. John Hope Franklin, in *The Militant South, 1800-1861* (Cambridge, Mass.: Harvard University Press, 1956), has amply documented this disposition. His bibliographical essay (pp. 251-64) is an excellent guide to the relevant sources. See also H.C. Brearley, "The Pattern of Violence," in W.T. Couch, ed., *Culture in the South* (Chapel Hill: University of North Carolina Press, 1934), pp. 685-89; Frank E. Vandiver, "The Southerner as Extremist," in Vandiver, ed., *The Idea of the South*, pp. 43-49; and Alfred O. Hero, Jr., *The Southerner and World Affairs* (Baton Rouge: Louisiana State University Press, 1965), pp. 78 ff.

4. Brearley, "Pattern of Violence," pp. 689-91; Vandiver, "Southerner as Extremist," pp. 49-55; W.J. Cash, *The Mind of the South* (New York: Alfred A. Knopf, 1941), pp. 115-26.

5. Cash, *Mind of the South*, pp. 115-26; Brearley, "Pattern of Violence," pp. 678-81; Arthur F. Raper, *The Tragedy of Lynching* (Chapel Hill: University of North Carolina Press, 1933).

6. Southern Commission on the Study of Lynching, *Lynchings and What They Mean* (Atlanta: The Commission, n.d.), p. 73.

7. "Pattern of Violence," p. 687. For similar observations a generation later, see Hodding Carter, *Southern Legacy* (Baton Rouge: Louisiana State University Press, 1950), pp. 48-63.

8. Hackney, "Southern Violence," pp. 906-08. See also Raymond D. Gastil, "Homicide and a Regional Culture of Violence," *American Sociological Review* 36 (June 1971): 412-27.

9. The poll is analyzed in Rodney Stark and James McEvoy III, "Middle-Class Violence," *Psychology Today* 4 (November 1970): 52-54, 110-12. By hypothesis, the South qualifies as a "subculture of violence": see Gastil, "Homicide and a Regional Culture of Violence"; and, for the concept, Marvin E. Wolfgang and Franco Ferracuti, "Subculture of Violence: An Integrated Conceptualization," in David O. Arnold, ed., *The Sociology of Subcultures* (Berkeley: The Glendessary Press, 1970), p. 147.

10. Albert J. Reiss, Jr. (with Otis Dudley Duncan, Paul K. Hatt, and Cecil C. North), *Occupations and Social Status* (Glencoe: Ill.: The Free Press, 1961), pp. 205, 211; Hero, *The Southerner and World Affairs*, pp. 80-103, 108 ff.; John Temple Graves, *The Fighting South* (New York: G.P. Putnam's Sons, 1943).

11. "Pattern of Violence," p. 678.

12. A study conducted by the Survey Research Center of the University of Michigan in 1959 and 1960 shows a similar regional difference in hunting. See Eva Mueller and Gerald Gurin, *Participation in Outdoor Recreation: Factors Affecting Demand among American Adults*, Outdoor Recreation Resources Review Commission Study Report 20 (Washington, D.C., 1962), p. 19.

13. Hackney, "Southern Violence," p. 919.

14. Ibid., pp. 919-20.

15. Quoted in Brearley, "Pattern of Violence," p. 678.

16. "Southern Violence," pp. 918-19.

17. AIPO 377, 1946.

18. AIPO 533, 1954; AIPO 538, 1954; AIPO 608, 1958; there were minor variations in question-wording.

19. *Grade Teacher*, September 1968, p. 152.

20. "Southern Violence," pp. 918-19. Hackney cites Martin Gold, "Suicide, Homicide, and the Socialization of Aggression," *American Journal of Sociology* 63 (May 1958): 651-61.

21. Raymond Tanter, "International War and Domestic Turmoil: Some Contemporary Evidence," in Hugh Davis Graham and Ted Robert Gurr, eds., *Violence in America: Historical and Comparative Perspectives*, Report to the National Commission on the Causes and Prevention of Violence (New York: Bantam Books, 1969), p. 555.

Chapter 6
"The Bible Belt": Southern Religion

1. "Religion in the South, Old and New," in McKinney and Thompson, eds., *The South in Continuity and Change*, p. 359. For a discussion of many of these observations, see Horace H. Cunningham, "The Southern Mind Since the Civil War," in Arthur S. Link and Rembert W. Patrick, eds., *Writing Southern History: Essays in Historiography in Honor of Fletcher M. Green* (Baton Rouge: Louisiana State University Press, 1965), pp. 386-92.

2. Mencken quoted in Tindall, *Emergence of the New South:* see pp. 208-10 for this and the Southern counter-attack; Cash, *Mind of the South*, p. 80.

3. *The Southern Tradition at Bay: A History of Postbellum Thought* (New Rochelle, N.Y.: Arlington House, 1968), p. 98. An historical account of the development of this solidarity can be found on pp. 98-111. See also Samuel S. Hill, Jr., *Southern Churches in Crisis* (New York: Holt, Rinehart and Winston, 1966), pp. 34-70; Fichter and Maddox, "Religion in the South," pp. 359 ff.; Hero, *The Southerner and World Affairs*, pp. 435-37.

4. Zelinsky, "An Approach to the Religious Geography of the United States: Patterns of Church Membership in 1952," *Annals of the Association of American Geographers* 51 (June 1961): 139-93; Samuel S. Hill, Jr., "An Agenda for Research on Religion," in Edgar T. Thompson, ed., *Perspectives on the South: Agenda for Research* (Durham: Duke University Press, 1967), p. 198. See also Hill, *Southern Churches in Crisis*, pp. 31-39, on the "Baptist-Methodist hegemony."

5. See the comparisons between Southern Baptists and "American" Baptists in Rodney Stark and Charles Y. Glock, *American Piety: The Nature of Religious Commitment* (Berkeley: University of California Press, 1968). Their sample comes from the Bay area of California, however, which may put the generalizability of their findings in question.

126

6. See Hero, *The Southerner and World Affairs*, pp. 435-41, 451 ff., 474, 491.

7. Ibid., p. 435.

8. "Religion in the South," p. 359.

9. Protestant-Catholic differences of many sorts are examined by Gerhard Lenski, in *The Religious Factor*, rev. ed. (Garden City, N.Y.: Anchor Books, Doubleday & Company, 1963), although his data are from a sample of Detroit Area residents, and Southern-born respondents are often specifically excluded (e.g., p. 109). For discussions of regional differences among Catholics and Jews, see Hero, *The Southerner and World Affairs*, pp. 451-503; Fichter and Maddox, "Religion in the South," pp. 369-82; Killian, *White Southerners*, pp. 69-83.

10. *Southern Tradition at Bay*, p. 98.

11. Edwin McNeill Poteat, Jr., "Religion in the South," in Couch, *Culture in the South*, p. 251.

12. "Southern Religion, Mid-Century," in Rubin and Kilpatrick, *The Lasting South*, p. 138.

13. AIPO 407, 1947. Quotes are from code categories in codebook supplied by Roper Center.

14. Poteat, "Religion in the South," p. 262; Francis Butler Simkins, "The Rising Tide of Faith," in Rubin and Kilpatrick, eds., *The Lasting South*, p. 94. See also Weaver, *Southern Tradition at Bay*, pp. 100-4.

15. AIPO 580, 1957.

16. Ibid.

17. *Southern Churches in Crisis*, p. 23.

18. Poteat, "Religion in the South," p. 261.

19. "The Rising Tide of Faith," p. 97.

20. Clement Eaton, *The Mind of the Old South*, rev. ed. (Baton Rouge: Louisiana State University Press, 1967), p. 203.

21. "Rising Tide of Faith," pp. 97-98.

22. Ibid., pp. 97-100; Tindall, *Emergence of the New South*, pp. 197-8. For the national situation, see Liston Pope, "Religion and the Class Structure," *Annals of The American Academy of Political and Social Science* 256 (March 1948): 84-91.

23. See, for example, Hill, *Southern Churches in Crisis*, p. 30; Simkins, "Rising Tide of Faith," pp. 95 ff.

24. Killian, *White Southerners*, pp. 69-83; Fichter and Maddox, "Religion in the South," p. 380.

25. See, for example, Hero, *The Southerner and World Affairs*, pp. 435-37; Fichter and Maddox, "Religion in the South," pp. 362-64.

26. "Rising Tide of Faith," pp. 87-88.

27. An AIPO press release of 11 April 1967, summarized in Stark and Glock, *American Piety*, p. 207, notes for the nation as a whole "a continuation of the downward trend in American church attendance which began in the late 1950s."

28. In ibid., pp. 86-89, it is observed that those most likely to listen to such services are also those most likely to attend.

29. AIPO 580, 1957.

30. NORC 294.

31. See, for example, Hill, *Southern Churches in Crisis*, p. 166; Brown, "Southern Religion, Mid-Century," pp. 138-39; Fichter and Maddox, "Religion in the South," p. 366; Cash, *The Mind of the South*, pp. 55-58.

32. AIPO 655, 1962.

33. AIPO 608, 1958; AIPO 721, 1965.

34. Fichter and Maddox, "Religion in the South," p. 365; Brown, "Southern Religion, Mid-Century," p. 138.

35. See also, for example, Hill, *Southern Churches in Crisis*, pp. 111-15; Cash, *Mind of the South*, pp. 58-60.

36. Do Cahalan, Ira H. Cisin, and Helen M. Crossley, *American Drinking Practices*, George Washington University Social Research Group Report No. 3, June 1967, pp. 51-52, 255, 258, 264, 285, 309, 315, 327, 331; Fichter and Maddox, "Religion in the South," p. 365; Hill, *Southern Churches in Crisis*, pp. 108-11.

37. AIPO 723, 1966; Cahalan et al., *American Drinking Practices*, pp. 327, 335.

38. *Sexual Behavior in the Human Female* (Philadelphia: W.B. Saunders Co., 1953), p. 36. A map on the same page indicates that nearly one-third of the "Southern" cases are Floridians.

39. AIPO 533, 1954. 48% disapprove in the South; 46% elsewhere.

40. On the role of the church in the slavery controversy, see, for example, Cash, *Mind of the South*, pp. 82-84; Weaver, *Southern Tradition at Bay*, pp. 208-13; Ulrich Bonnell Phillips, *The Course of the South to Secession* (New York: Hill and Wang, 1964), p. 103; or Seymour Martin Lipset, "Religion and Politics in the American Past and Present," in Robert Lee and Martin Marty, eds., *Religion and Social Conflict* (New York: Oxford University Press, 1964), pp. 79 ff. For the later controversies, see Kenneth K. Bailey, *Southern White Protestantism in the Twentieth Century* (New York: Harper and Row, 1964), esp. pp. 72-110.

41. "Religion in the South," p. 383. For discussions of the official denominational positions, actions at the congregational level, and the frequent discrepancies between them, see Clyde L. Manschreck, "Religion in the South: Problem and Promise," in Francis B. Simkins, ed., *The South in Perspective* (Farmville, Va.: Longwood College, 1959), esp. pp. 81-90; Bailey, *Southern White Protestantism*, pp. 130-58; Clark, *The Emerging South*, pp. 248-70; Hill, *Southern Churches in Crisis*, passim.

42. *The South and the Southerner* (Boston: Little, Brown & Company, 1959), p. 270.

43. See, for instance, Raymond C. Rymph and Jeffrey K. Hadden, "The Per-

sistence of Regionalism in Racial Attitudes of Methodist Clergy," *Social Forces* 49 (September 1970): 41-50.

44. For the former, see Bailey, *Southern White Protestantism*, pp. 152-54, 159-67; Simkins, "Rising Tide of Faith," pp. 90-96; Manschreck, "Religion in the South," pp. 84-89. For the latter, see, for instance, McGill, *The South and the Southerner*, pp. 274-80; or James W. Silver, *Mississippi: The Closed Society*, enl. ed. (New York: Harcourt, Brace, & World, 1966), pp. 53-60. A relevant case study by two social scientists, Ernest Campbell and Thomas Pettigrew, is *Christians in Racial Crisis: A Study of Little Rock's Ministry* (Washington: Public Affairs Press, 1959).

45. "Religion in the South," p. 89. See also Simkins, "Rising Tide of Faith," pp. 90-96.

46. Cash, *Mind of the South*, p. 79.

47. *Southern Churches in Crisis*, p. 29.

48. Glenn and Simmons, in "Are Regional Cultural Differences Diminishing?"—analyzing some of the same items used here—arrive at the same conclusion by a somewhat different route. Cf. the results of studies conducted for the *Catholic Digest* by NORC in 1952 and 1965, reported in Martin E. Marty, Stuart E. Rosenberg, and Andrew M. Greeley, *What Do We Believe?: The Stance of Religion in America* (New York: Meredith Press, 1968), pp. 178-346.

Chapter 7
The Enduring South

1. Richard L. Simpson, discussion of Glenn and Simmons, "Are Regional Cultural Differences Diminishing?" at the Convention of the American Sociological Association, 1965.

2. Broom and Glenn, "Negro-White Differences in Reported Attitudes and Behavior," *Sociology and Social Research* 50 (January 1966): 187 (abst.), 189. The description of the items, which Glenn has used in several articles, is taken from Glenn and Simmons, "Are Regional Cultural Differences Diminishing?" p. 178. The strategy of assessing the importance of a difference by comparing it to another which is already conceded to be important is suggested in Hyman, *Survey Design and Analysis*, pp. 189-92.

3. "Massification versus Differentiation: Some Trend Data from National Surveys," *Social Forces* 46 (December 1967): 172-80, especially table 1, p. 176.

4. *The Uncertain South: Its Changing Patterns of Politics in Foreign Policy* (Chicago: Quadrangle Books, 1964), p. 236. On the *ecological* differences between Northern and Southern cities, see Gordon Blackwell, "The Changing South," in Simkins, ed., *The South in Perspective*, pp. 22-23; and various articles in Rupert B. Vance and Nicholas J. Demerath, eds., *The Urban South* (Chapel Hill: University of North Carolina Press, 1954).

5. "Massification versus Differentiation," p. 172 (abst.).

6. W.M. Frohock, quoted in Westbrook, "Twilight of Southern Regionalism," p. 232.

7. Alfred O. Hero, Jr., *The Southerner and World Affairs*, pp. 351-55.

8. T.W. Adorno et al., *The Authoritarian Personality* (New York: Harper and Brothers, 1950), esp. pp. 255-57, 759-62, 794-800.

9. See Herbert H. Hyman and Paul B. Sheatsley, "The Authoritarian Personality—A Methodological Critique," in Richard Christie and Marie Jahoda, eds., *Studies in the Scope and Method of "The Authoritarian Personality,"* (Glencoe, Ill.: The Free Press, 1954), pp. 104-15; Richard Christie and John Garcia, "Subcultural Variation in Authoritarian Personality," *Journal of Abnormal and Social Psychology* 46 (October 1951): 457-69; E. Terry Prothro and Levon Melikian, "The California Public Opinion Scale in an Authoritarian Culture," *Public Opinion Quarterly* 17 (Fall 1953): 353-62.

10. "Are Regional Cultural Differences Diminishing?" pp. 183-87.

11. Computed from figures presented ibid., pp. 183-87. The authors' analysis is based on forty-four items, but they present data only for the thirty-four items which show more than "negligible interage difference in [regional] variation" (p. 181).

12. See the review article by L. Paul Metzger, "American Sociology and Black Assimilation: Conflicting Perspectives," *American Journal of Sociology* 76 (January 1971): 627-47. See also Clyde V. Kiser, "Cultural Pluralism," *Annals of the American Academy of Political and Social Science* 262 (March 1949): 117-30; or Nathan Glazer and Daniel Patrick Moynihan, *Beyond the Melting Pot* (Cambridge: M. I. T. Press, 1963), esp. pp. 12-20.

13. NORC 341/342. "Don't know" responses excluded. Emphasis in the original interview schedule.

14. See, for instance, Edward Zigler and Irvin L. Child, "Socialization," in Gardner Lindzey and Elliot Aronson, eds., *Handbook of Social Psychology*, 2nd ed. 5 vols. (Reading, Mass.: Addison-Wesley Publishing Company, 1969), 3: 450-589, esp. pp. 474-501. Although there has been extensive research on social class differences in child-rearing, as the review by Zigler and Child indicates, there has been virtually none on *regional* variation—which the present data indicate to be substantial.

15. Center for Southern Education Studies, Division of Surveys and Field Services, *High Schools in the South: A Fact Book* (Nashville: George Peabody College for Teachers, 1966), p. 90.

16. *AAUP Bulletin* 53, no. 3 (September 1967): 268. See also Samuel A. Stouffer, *Communism, Conformity, and Civil Liberties: A Cross-section of the Nation Speaks Its Mind* (Garden City, N.Y.: Doubleday & Company, 1955), pp. 109-30.

17. M. Kent Jennings and Harmon Zeigler, "Political Expressivism among High School Teachers: The Intersection of Community and Occupational

Values," in Roberta S. Sigel, ed., *Learning About Politics: A Reader in Political Socialization* (New York: Random House, [1970]), pp. 434-53.

18. Reiss et al., *Occupations and Social Status*, pp. 199, 205; Glenn and Simmons, "Are Regional Cultural Differences Diminishing?" p. 185.

19. "Comparative Newspaper Handling of the Emmett Till Case," *Journalism Quarterly* 35 (Summer 1958): 291-98.

20. Ibid., p. 298. Much of the discussion in Herbert H. Hyman and Paul B. Sheatsley, "Some Reasons Why Information Campaigns Fail," *Public Opinion Quarterly* 11 (Fall 1947): 413-23, is relevant, allowing for the fact that the "message" in this case is not composed of information.

21. Dick Hobson, "Who Watches What?" *TV Guide*, 27 July 1968, p. 6.

22. Reiss et al., *Occupations and Social Status*, pp. 207-8.

23. "Massification versus Differentiation," p. 172 (abst.)

24. Ruth C. Schaffer and Albert Schaffer, "Socialization and the Development of Attitudes toward Negroes in Alabama," *Phylon* 27 (Fall 1966): 274-85, esp. table on p. 282; Hyman and Sheatsley, "Attitudes toward Desegregation."

25. *Constructing Social Theories* (New York: Harcourt, Brace & World, 1968), pp. 101 ff.

26. "The Quest for the Central Theme in Southern History," paper read at Conference of the Southern Historical Association, 1962.

27. For critical summaries of this literature, see ibid.; D. Potter, *The South and the Sectional Conflict*, esp. pp. 3-33; and Tindall, "Mythology: A New Frontier in Southern History," pp. 1-15. Much of the material has been collected in Dewey W. Grantham, ed., *The South and the Sectional Image: The Sectional Theme Since Reconstruction* (New York: Harper and Row, 1967) and in Monroe L. Billington, ed., *The South: A Central Theme?* (New York: Holt, Rinehart and Winston, 1969). The modern quest was begun by U.B. Phillips, with his paper, "The Central Theme of Southern History," 1928.

28. C. Vann Woodward, "The Irony of Southern History," *Journal of Southern History* 19 (1953): 13.

29. Lerche, *The Uncertain South*, p. 243.

30. Hackney, "Southern Violence," pp. 924-25. See the similar catalogue in Lerche, *The Uncertain South*, pp. 245 ff.

31. Karl Marx and Frederick Engels, *The Civil War in the United States*, Centennial Edition (New York: The Citadel Press, 1961), p. 72.

32. Hackney, "Southern Violence," p. 925; Lerche, *The Uncertain South*, p. 243. Cf. Vandiver, "The Southerner as Extremist." For an especially pertinent theoretical discussion, see Lewis A.Coser, *The Functions of Social Conflict* (London: Free Press of Glencoe, 1964).

33. Compare Philippe Garigue, "The French-Canadian Family," in Mason Wade, ed., *Canadian Dualism: Studies of French-English Relations* (Toronto: University of Toronto Press, 1960), pp. 181-200.

34. Hackney, "Southern Violence," pp. 924-25.

35. See Stinchcombe, *Constructing Social Theories*, pp. 103-08.

36. Hero, *The Southerner and World Affairs*, pp. 78-138.

37. "From the First Reconstruction to the Second," p. 14.

38. Poster of the Great Southern Circus, quoted in E. Merton Coulter, *College Life in the Old South* (Athens: University of Georgia Press, 1951), p. 223.

Index

About the Author

John Shelton Reed is Assistant Professor of Sociology and a Research Associate of the Institute for Research in Social Science at the University of North Carolina at Chapel Hill. A Tennesseean, he is a graduate of the Massachusetts Institute of Technology in political science and mathematics and received his Ph.D. in sociology from Columbia University.